SCULPT & TONE

YOUR CURVES

SCULPT & TONE
YOUR CURVES

First Edition
ISBN: 9781916198319

Published by
DreamBody Fitness

Printed in the United Kingdom
10 9 8 7 6 5 4 3 2 1

Library of Congress Cataloging-in-Publication Data

Contents
AT A GLANCE

TABLE OF *Contents*

Welcome

**Welcome to The Ultimate Fitness Model Body tTansformation Guide.
I am so excited to get you started on your DreamGirl journey!**

Within this easy to read guidebook, you'll learn the simple outline and steps you can take to create a **healthier**, **curvier**, **stronger**, and **sexier** body. Better yet, you'll discover how to achieve maximum results, without any extremes.

While this is not a comprehensive guide, I've written it so it covers the fundamentals and puts into context how a successful body transformation really works, without losing precious muscle and without hitting a fat loss plateau.

WELCOME TO THE DREAMGIRL TEAM

"

If you don't sacrifice for

What you want

What you want becomes the

Sacrifice

Escaping the

Skinny fat

epidemic

"

F*ck skinny
Get
sexy

From soft and shapeless to
tight and toned

my experience

MY *humble* beginnings

Throughout my life I have always appeared slim, but I was also fat.

That boggled my brain. I mean, being slim means looking tight and toned too, right? Apparently not because I definitely didn't have any tone, and I was far from tight.

Sure I fitted into the smallest garments, weighed only 115 lbs, was well within healthy BMI readings, and was what many people strive to achieve, but I hated my body because it looked soft and squidgy, I had zero definition and I even considered investing in a back bra to conceal the rolls that clung to my rear? Eww. I was so unhappy, and I wanted more.

I wanted to wear a bikini, and feel good about myself

This was me

but I was stuck in
skinny fat limbo land

The land where you're too slim for anyone to give a damn,
but fat enough that you look plain wrong in a swimsuit,
and let's just forget sexy lingerie.

Sigh.

I became that girl who knew how to strategically wear clothing that would camouflage and downplay my bodily flaws. In came the black and boring, and out went the slim fitting and elegant.

Whenever I did share my concerns, my friends would proclaim *"You look great hun, I'd kill for your body"* and my family would plead *"You don't need a diet, you're already so slim".*

I'm sure they thought I harboured some sort of eating disorder.Unfortunately, the only disorder I had was a body image one.

I felt so lost. At least if I was obviously overweight there would be someone to help, but I was alone in my skinny fat body.

The only people that understood my heartache were those who were suffering the same fate, but they were just as confused as I was. Some had even given up hope, putting it down to wrong genetics and believing that some people just aren't destined for a tight and toned body.

But thankfully I wasn't ready to give up...

Dazed and Confused.

Dazed and confused by what appeared to be some sort of psychological curse, I became convinced that all I needed to do was lose a bit more weight. That if I could just eliminate all my body fat, I would sport a perfectly toned body that would be ready to grace beaches worldwide and, of course, leave hot guys drooling in my wake.

And so, in 2008, spurred on by flawed and faulty fitness hype and marketing scams ,I donned a shiny new pair of running shoes, popped my first thermogenic fat burning compound, and began my quest for a hot beach body. I was ready

Start here

AND SO...
...the quest *began*

I was totally hyped and determined to reach my goal. I dropped all carbohydrates from my diet, was consuming the baseline 1200 calories, and took up running 5 miles a day, every day. **Nothing** was going to stand in my way.

As I got fitter, I introduced some resistance and HIIT training into my routine for good measure, and upped my running game to 10 miles on 2 out of the 7 days.

For several months I slaved away in my home gym, running through painful shin splints and doing hundreds of sit ups, awaiting the day I would unveil my leaner, sexier body.

...IT WAS MY RECIPE FOR METABOLIC DISASTER

4 months of hard work, low calories and low carbs, and this is what I ended up with.

I WAS TOTALLY *heartbroken*

...only now I was worse off than when I started.

Now I had a damaged metabolism, my hormones were completely out of whack, and I lost a significant amount of precious muscle along with all my hopes for a dream body.

As quickly as I lost the weight, it came pouring back on, back fat and all. I was in the worst shape of my life and spiraling downwards.

I COULDN'T STOP *piling on* THE LB'S, AND THEN THIS HAPPENED...

I got even *fatter*!!!

I HAD ENTERED THE VICIOUS *Weight loss* CYCLE

And fueled my skinny fat syndrome

under the guidance of conventional flawed fitness wisdom.

If you are relating to any part of my story, take heed because my journey didn't end there and, now that you are a DreamGirl, yours won't either.

So keep reading...

AND THEN IT *Happened*

THE *turning point* CAME

So, what did happen next and how did things turn around?

After this dreadful experience, I got really angry. I vowed I would never put my body through a flawed and faulty weight loss program ever again. Then the turning point came, I got serious.

Serious about education, and serious about doing things right. For the next 7 years, I learnt all I could about my skinny fat syndrome, how to change my body composition, I hired a physique coach and I experimented with new strategies. I even studied and achieved several qualifications to bolster my learning.

Finally, this happened.
I done it

The Best bit...

I managed to drop the body fat without extreme dieting or deprivation, and

It took just

16 Weeks

to go from skinny fat to tight and toned

How did I do it?
This is what DreamCurves will teach you

MY *Proudest* Moment

In October 2015, I stepped on stage within the
bikini division of a bodybuilding contest.

The proudest
moment of my
life

I managed to reduce my unsightly body fat and I had definition from the
hard earned muscle I had developed. I was in the best shape of my life,
and not an ounce of back fat in sight.

My 16 week Progress

BE *fearless* IN THE PURSUIT

OF WHAT SETS YOUR *soul*

ON *fire*

Let's get *Started* ...

During the process of leaning down for the stage, and since my glitzy bikini debut, I have gained a wealth of knowledge and experience that have enabled me to further perfect my strategy for breaking out of the skinny fat cycle once and for all, and develop the hottest, leanest, tightest body with curves to die for.

And that is the process that I will now share with you.

So, let's get to it.

What exactly is

Skinny fat

syndrome?

Skinny Fat Syndrome

A skinny fat person often looks slim, healthy and falls within normal BMI parameters, however, their body fat is out of proportion to their lean muscle mass, resulting in a soft appearance that lacks tone and volume.

This is the reason why skinny fat is also termed 'normal weight obesity'.

Skinny Fat

Skinny Fat

Skinny Fat

Skinny Fat

As you can see in these photos, each lady is slim and would look great in clothing, but they lack the muscular structure that gives them tone and definition.

THE SCARY THING IS MANY FEMALES ARE HEADING FOR THIS *without* REALISING IT

What *Causes* it?

This soft appearance is caused by an imbalanced body composition which, put simply, means **having too much fat** and **too little muscle**.

Unfortunately, these results are typical of conventional one size fits all weight loss programs.

Skinny fat is typically the result of:

+ Inefficient or lack of weight training
+ Too much cardio
+ Inactive lifestyle
+ Fad dieting

If any of those circumstances describe you and you are a slim build with a soft appearance, chances are you are skinny fat.

While that isn't what you want to hear, the good news is skinny fat syndrome is reversible and **you are on the right program to do that.**

" "

Train like a *beast*

Look like a

Beauty

How to
Transform
your body

Body recomposition

Skinny fat is a horrible place to be and most females will confuse their soft exterior with being fat and run straight for fat loss programs.

Yes fat loss will be necessary to achieve a tight and toned body, however, there is a difference between being fat and being soft, and this is where the confusion lies and frustration occurs.

Unfortunately, there are a lot of fitness guru's that mistakingly prescribe conventional weight loss programs to us skinny fat gals, not realising that weight loss is not necessarily what we need.

Allow me to elaborate a bit further...

Your body composition is a vital component in achieving tight and toned curves. The images on the following page demonstrate just how vital this is.. While both ladies are obviously slim, you can clearly see that the lady on the right has much more muscular structure.

If you have a low level of muscle mass, you're going to have to diet down hard and get super lean to lose the skinny fat appearance. As you can imagine, this is not healthy, it's not fun and it isn't sustainable.

Worse still, because you lack muscle, you'll have nothing to give you the shape and definition you are aiming for, so all you'll reveal after all that hard work is a bony structure that leaves you looking frail and starved. Ugh, not exactly what you had in mind I'm sure.

Weight loss *vs* body recomposition

Conventional weight loss

Body recomp

... and see what it does to the shape of your *booty* ... *oo la la*

The shape of your butt is directly related to the strength of your glutes.

Weak, unused, neglected glutes are going to give you a saggy and flat butt, that lacks depth and fullness. A pair of glutes that are in shape, strengthened and well trained, however, will look very different.

They will be perky, round and shapely.

And what is the ultimate difference between the two? .

Muscle. It's all about muscle.

SKINNY FAT

MUSCLE

The *upsides* are *endless* ....

Muscle is very metabolic, meaning that you'll burn more calories making it easier to drop fat, and keep it off.

Better still, if you do put on some fat through over indulgences, which we all do once in a while, muscle looks great even with a few fatty pounds covering it.

Muscle is a *win-win*

And there are many more upsides to increasing your muscle mass.

Weight training *vs* cardio

Have you ever noticed how many people slog away on the cardio machines in the gym, or take every aerobics class available? And yet have you also noticed how their bodies never seem to change?

Unfortunately, these people are just following the age old flawed advice of doing lots of cardio to lose weight.

I'm not saying cardio is bad or wrong.

The problem is, many people don't understand the concept of body composition, and they certainly don't understand how to use cardio in the right way.

Here are some of the problems with

Cardio exercise

1. Long sessions are counterproductive to muscle growth

2. Too much cardio leads to muscle loss

3. Cardio can stress the body, leading to back fat and muffin top

4. Cardio makes you hungry, which may lead to eating back the calories or feeling deprived

5. The body adapts to increase efficiency, resulting in less calories being burned

Why training with weights is *best*

Weight training is a body composition and sculpting tool which, conveniently, also includes all the fat loss benefits of cardio exercise. However, weight training has benefits far and beyond those gained from cardio.

Let's take a brief look at some of those.

✓ Improvements in body composition means a leaner and tighter body

✓ Targeted weight training causes changes in body shape and enhances feminine curves

✓ More muscle mass means increased resting metabolic rate

✓ An increased metabolic rate means maintenance is easier

✓ Weight training increases calorie burn post training

✓ Heavy lifting burns more energy, making it effective for fat loss

✓ Weightlifting helps preserve lean mass while restricting calories for fat loss

✓ Posture is improved

✓ Cellulite is diminished

And much more besides

Use cardio to *supplement* your training, **not** as the primary focus

Cardio exercise is a great fat loss tool when used correctly and in conjunction with a structured weight training program. However, if your goal is to carve out a tight and toned bikini body with plenty of sexy curves, then cardio exercise is better used as a supplement to weight training, not the primary focus.

When it comes to body composition, **there is such a thing as too much cardio**, so the key is to use it in a way that minimises muscle loss and maximises fat loss. How much cardio you need is ultimately determined by how lean you are, how lean you are looking to get, and your genetics.

It all comes down to

what *outcome* **you** want to create

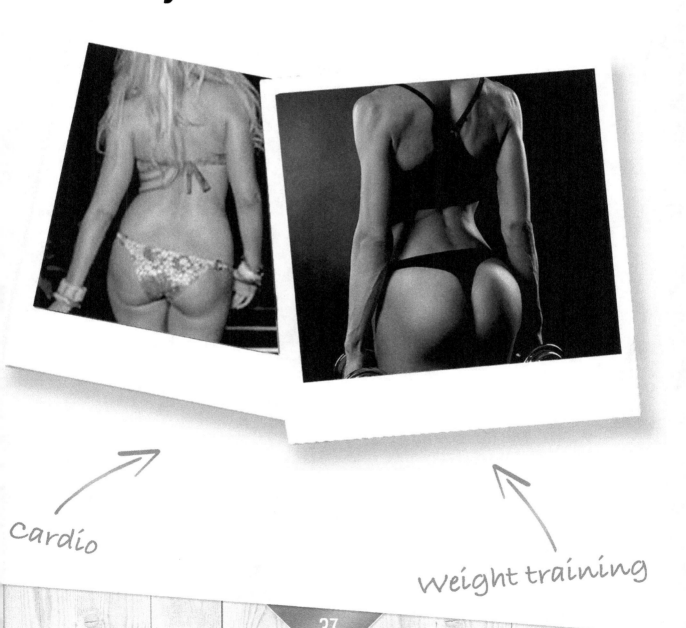

Cardio

Weight training

The Deadly Combo

When trying to reduce body fat, most people increase cardio and lower their calories. When you're in a caloric deficit, your body is already primed for muscle loss. Add to this low carbs and cardio on an empty stomach and **say goodbye to your beautiful muscle and hello skinny fat syndrome**.

How and why does this happen?

After a certain point, energy from your food becomes exhausted. At this point your body seeks a new source of energy to maintain it's requirements and keep you moving.

Sure, part of this supply is from fat storage, but it also begins to metabolise your muscle along with it. Worse still, in a drastic caloric deficit, the body shifts to starvation mode. This is where **fat is spared for life preservation, and muscle is shed** because it is calorie consuming.

At this point, the weight loss you see reflected back on the scales is partially at the expense of precious muscle.

The outcome of being in a
calorie deficit, doing too
much cario and doing no
weight training

When working on fat reduction, some muscle loss is inevitable, so the goal is to maintain as much lean mass and strength as possible, while maximising fat burning potential.

There are *five key elements* that will help you offset the muscle burn effect as you slim down, these are:

- ❤ REDUCE CARDIO TO SHORTER AND MORE INTENSE HIIT SESSIONS

- ❤ SUPPLEMENT WITH AMINO ACID (BCAA) DRINKS BEFORE OR DURING CARDIO

- ❤ USE A MODERATE CALORIE DEFICIT

- ❤ HAVE ADEQUATE PROTEIN

- ❤ FOCUS ON LIFTING HEAVY WEIGHTS

"

Imagine yourself

6 months

from now

Oo la la

Concerns

about the recomp process

Ignore the *flawed* and *faulty* fitness advice

Body recomposition can seem like a scary process because there are far too many misunderstandings and flawed approaches circulating that have put females off weight training.

Going through a successful body recomposition process requires ignoring advice given by mainstream media and some fitness gurus, and being willing to start over with

A *fresh* PERSPECTIVE

In particular, you're going to have to ditch your reliance on the scales and alter your view on weight lifting and developing muscles because here's the bottom line...

Whatever your genetics, if you want to totally transform your body from skinny fat to tight and toned, you need to build muscle and, in order to build muscle, you need to lift heavy weights.

It's that simple.

So, with that said, let's take a look at the common concerns women have about the process and dispel those misconceptions once and for all.

Getting Bulky

What GIRLS think weights will do

What weights will ACTUALLY do

I'll be honest with you getting bulky is a real and completely logical concern. It is entirely possible to get bulky if you follow mindless muscle building programs that pick out a list of exercises and machines, without regard for your individual body shape and the outcome being created.

The key is to train your body according to your needs and with emphasis on creating balanced and streamlined proportions.

Within this guide, I will teach you what exercises will work best for you and what exercises to avoid, resulting in some very *sexy* and *feminine* curves that are in proportion to your body shape.

ABSOLUTELY *no bulking*

As for getting too big, most people don't realise the shear amount of work that goes into gaining muscular size, let alone the fact that us females just aren't genetically built to gain lots of size without the use of synthetic enhancements.

Just sexy feminine curves

The images you see of muscle bound women is the result of several hours of training per day, years of hard work and some use of enhancements. But don't fear, I promise I'll not be promoting any such drugs on this program, and you certainly won't be training for endless hours.

Now, let's say for arguments sake that you're a genetically superior miracle who does grow muscles like weeds. You are in control of how you use this program and that means you can also use your initiative to pull back if you desire. In fact, I encourage you to use your initiative because I want you to learn all you can during this program.

Having said that, I also want you to trust in the process and be able to distinguish between your fear versus the reality.

HERE'S THE *funny thing*

As a newbie to training, your body will develop muscle a bit faster than someone accustomed to training, but that'll soon slow down and, trust me, when you discover how muscle can transform the appearance of your body for the better, you'll be pleading for them to grow faster.

Getting big or bulky is not a problem with this program, unless you consider firm rounded glutes, shapely shoulders and killer legs too bulky. I sure hope not.

Scale *Weight*

UH OH! I GAINED A POUND. GASP

Okay, I'm being a little facetious there, but far too many people get so wrapped up in weight loss that they don't consider where that weight is coming from and end up losing precious lean muscle mass, thus continuing the skinny fat cycle.

If you are worried about weight gain, now is the time to adjust that thinking because you will more than likely put on some weight during a recomposition process. Why is this? Because muscle is denser and heavier than fat, and the goal is to increase muscle, not to mention that hydration levels fluctuate daily.

This is why having some knowledge about how a body recomposition process works is crucial to your sanity.

AS YOU SEE YOUR BODY GETTING *tight* AND *toned*

THOSE PESKY SCALES WILL NO LONGER BOTHER YOU

WEIGHT IS MEANINGLESS

As you begin gaining lean muscle, there may be some weeks where the number on the scales don't budge, or you may even find your weight increase slightly. If you have any hang ups on the number reflected back at you, a body recomposition process will surely be a stressful one.

Scales do have their place, and we will be using them as part of this process, however, weight gain is not something to be feared when it is coming from lean body mass. In fact, it is to be celebrated because **more muscle means an increase in your metabolism** and you'll burn more calories while at rest.

We do use scales within this program, but we use them alongside a variety of tools so we can better understand where the progress being made. There are no guessing games with this program.

And please have faith. You'll be rocking a super hot bikini body in no time if you trust the process. I know you may be feeling somewhat worried right now, but **I absolutely promise you that you will love the results.**

I PROMISE YOU'LL *love* THE RESULTS

I'm not B.S'ing you or trying to make a quick buck out of your misfortune. This program gets real results.

less of this

FAT ONE POUND MUSCLE

more of this

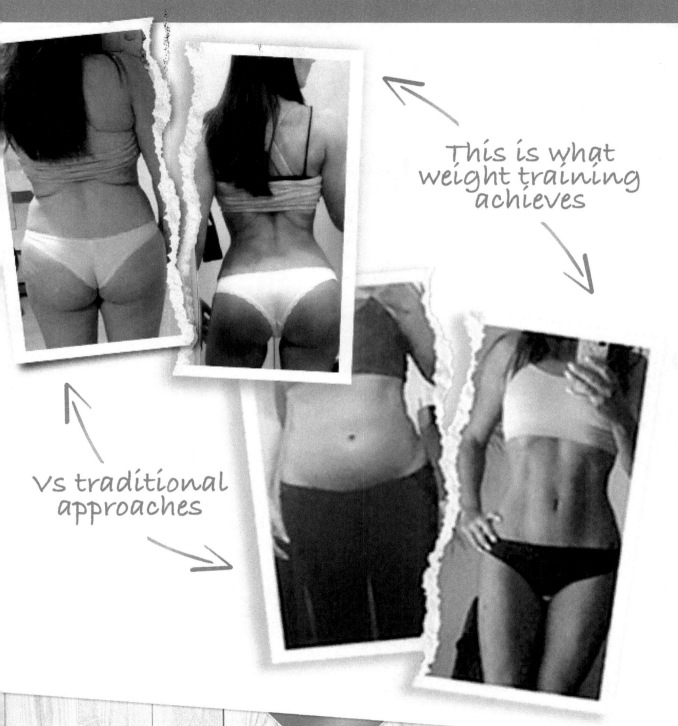

This is what
weight training
achieves

vs traditional
approaches

GETTING *fat*

Similar to the fear of getting big and bulky or putting on weight, women are afraid of getting fat, so they skimp on calories and wonder why they end up looking soft and skinny, with zero signs of definition.

Here's the thing ladies, you need to eat in order to grow muscle, so the key is to eat and train correctly and consistently so that those calories are used to build your muscles and are not syphoned off to your love handles or saddlebags.

KEEP FAT UNDER CONTROL WITH THESE GUIDELINES

- ❤ TRAIN HEAVY TO INCREASE INSULIN SENSITIVITY
- ❤ PERFORM HIGH INTENSITY INTERVAL CARDIO (aka HIIT)
- ❤ USE CALORIE AND CARB CYCLING STRATEGIES
- ❤ KEEP CARBS AROUND YOUR TRAINING
- ❤ AVOID EATING TO EXCESS OR OVER-INDULGING ON RE-FEED MEALS

Now that we've determined that muscle is good, the next question to pop up is:

IS IT POSSIBLE TO *build muscle* AND *lose fat* AT THE SAME TIME?

The answer is not as simple as yes or no because it depends on your starting point and your genetics.

There are three basic body types, these are

♥ **Ectomorph** (loses fat easily, but tends to struggle to gain muscle)

♥ **Endomorph** (gains muscle readily, but tends to struggle to lose fat)

♥ **Mesomorph** (loses fat and gains muscle readily)

An endomorph or mesomorph body type will tend to develop muscle more readily than ectomorphs, so this will be a factor in your rate of muscle growth and ability to be in a deficit while gaining that muscle.

Also, if you are new to training or lifting heavy, you'll grow muscle much more readily within the first 2-6 months. This is called newbie gains and is the best time to see muscle growth while in a caloric deficit.

Over time, your body will begin to adapt to regular training, your initial progress begins to slow and it becomes increasingly difficult to develop muscle. At this point, growing muscle within a deficit will become more and more of a challenge.

HOW HEAVY SHOULD YOU *lift*?

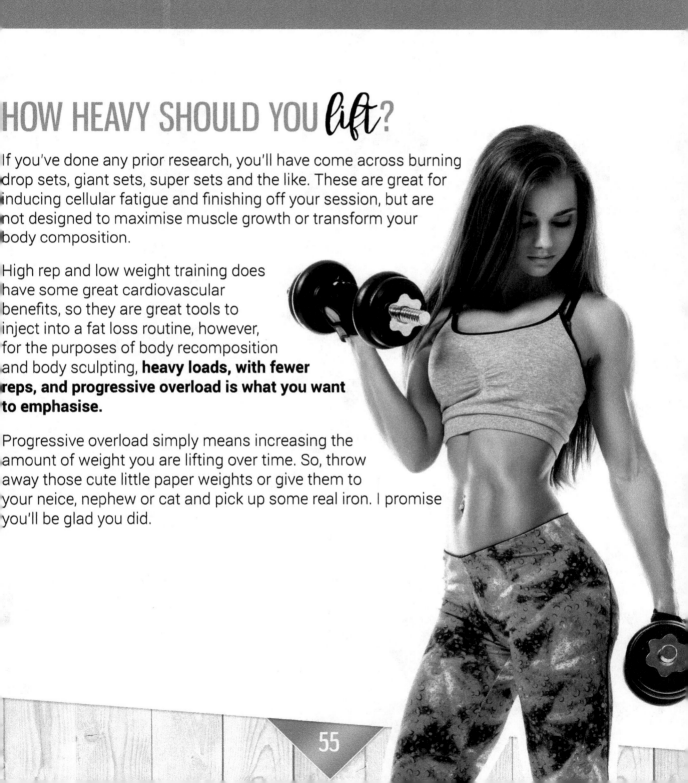

If you've done any prior research, you'll have come across burning drop sets, giant sets, super sets and the like. These are great for inducing cellular fatigue and finishing off your session, but are not designed to maximise muscle growth or transform your body composition.

High rep and low weight training does have some great cardiovascular benefits, so they are great tools to inject into a fat loss routine, however, for the purposes of body recomposition and body sculpting, **heavy loads, with fewer reps, and progressive overload is what you want to emphasise.**

Progressive overload simply means increasing the amount of weight you are lifting over time. So, throw away those cute little paper weights or give them to your neice, nephew or cat and pick up some real iron. I promise you'll be glad you did.

"

Skinny Girls look
good in clothes
Fit Girls look
good
Naked

Get ready to

Sculpt

hourglass
curves

"

If you keep doing
what you've always
done,you'll only
get what you've
always got

How to make
adjustments for your

Body Type

and enhance your results

The *three* body types

As covered briefly in an earlier section, there are three basic body types, these are

♥ Ectomorph ♥ Mesomorph ♥ Endomorph

ECTOMORPH

FAST METABOLISM
STRUGGLES TO GAIN
MUSCLE OR FAT

MESOMORPH

EFFICIENT METABOLISM
GAINS MUSCLE AND LOSES
FAT WITH RELATIVE EASE
WELL PROPORTIONED

ENDOMORPH

SLIGGISH METABOLISM
GAINS FAT EASILY AND HAS
DIFFICULTY LOSING AND
KEEPING FAT OFF

These body types are based on your bodies propensity for fat and muscle gain and frame size. Depending on your body type, you may respond better to one type of exercise and diet over another.

Knowing and understanding this will make it easier to achieve the results you want. So let's take a deeper look at each.

Mesomorphs are often referred to as genetically *gifted*

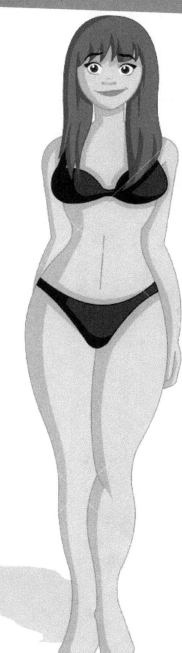

They have efficient metabolisms, so don't have to worry too much about what they eat, and they tend to be relatively muscular without much effort, which gives them an athletic and strong appearance, and excellent definition.

They tend to be well proportioned all over, tending to store fat evenly throughout their bodies. They are often characterised by strong bones, thick thighs, and appear blessed with curves.

💜 **Medium size joints and bones**

💜 **Naturally lean and lose fat readily**

💜 **Natrually muscular and gain shape easily**

💜 **Naturally strong and responds well to exercise**

💜 **Have plenty of curves and shape**

As this body type gains muscle relatively easily, care should be taken to introduce the correct targeted weight training, so not to increase muscular size in the wrong areas.

The good news is that sculpting out a super sexy feminine shape will be easiest for this body type.

Ectomorphs are *blessed* with efficient metabolisms

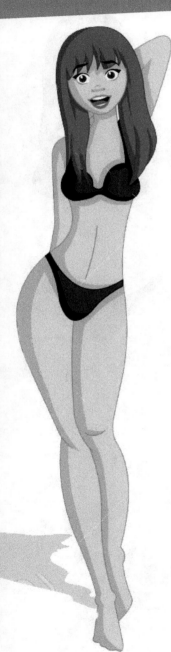

Ectomorphs tend to be naturally slim and wiry. They have difficulties in gaining weight and adding lean mus mass, even without exercising and dieting.

Ectomorphs are often flat chested, lack curves and are slightly boyish in shape.

Models, ballerina's and basketball players are characteri of ectomorph qualities, which can be defined as:

- ♥ **Slim joints and bones**
- ♥ **Fragile and delicate bodies**
- ♥ **Long limbs**
- ♥ **Linear body shape**
- ♥ **Small shoulders**
- ♥ **Small chest and buttocks**
- ♥ **Little muscle mass**

FOCUS ON *Sculpting* CURVES

The focus of this body type is on gaining lean muscle mass and sculpting out the curves of your petite frame.

The good news is body fat will remain naturally low, so you'll be able to eat in a more relaxed manner and any new definition will be immediately visible.

The bad news, you'll have to work hard to sculpt those curves.

Limit cardio as much as possible, and you'll certainly want to avoid HIIT routines. Launch full steam ahead into a muscle building program and lift heavy.

Also be wary of undereating or restricting your carbohydrates.

Endomorphs are *blessed* with curves

Endomorphs have a sluggish metabolism so gain weight relatively easily and, therefore, tend to appear soft and curvy.

That being said, endomorphs also gain muscle easily, so an in shape endomorph appears very feminine and sexy with plenty of curves.

- ♥ **Medium to large joints and frame**
- ♥ **Smooth and round body**
- ♥ **Short limbs**
- ♥ **Higher levels of body fat**
- ♥ **Gains muscle and fat easily**
- ♥ **Loses fat slowly**

FOCUS ON KEEPING
Body Fat UNDER CONTROL

Because an endomorphs metabolism is unforgiving, the focus is primarily on lowering body fat levels. This can be achieved through HIIT training, a lower intake of carbohydrates and maintaining a calorie deficit even during the muscle building phase.

You'll also find that as you develop more lean tissue, your metabolism will increase. So lift those heavy weights.

The good news is that sculpting a beautiful and sexy hourglass shape will be easy for you.

The bad news, you'll have to work hard to show off those curves.

"

Sculpt a

Bad Ass Body

One *curve* at a
time

How to transform any

Body Shape

Five body *shapes*

Which *shape* are you?

Which *shape* are you?

As you are no doubt aware, there are five basic body shapes. These are:

- ♥ Hourglass
- ♥ Inverted Triangle
- ♥ Pear (aka triangle)
- ♥ Ruler (aka rectangle)
- ♥ Apple (aka round)

Understanding your basic shape is fundamental to bringing balance to your proportions and sculpting the hourglass shape.

It may not be what you *think*

It is possible that bloating, water retention, body fat and hormones are masking your true underlying shape

If your excess body fat goes straight to your hips and thighs for instance, you may appear to be pear shaped, where in fact you may be hourglass beneath it all. Similarly, if your hormones are a bit out of balance, you may appear to be an apple shape.

What we're interested in here is the underlying bone and muscular structure.

To determine your shape, strip down to your underwear and look at yourself straight on in the mirror. Place your hands and arms a little away from your sides, and legs together.

Examine the area under your arms, your bust and ribcage, your waist and hips, and determine the fullest part. Don't be afraid to poke and prod the area to see how much is body fat vs bone and muscular structure.

Take a look at the following pages to determine the closest match. It is possible to fall between the shapes and body fat may distort the perception, so a bit of judgement from you will be needed. A rough guess is fine as you'll be able to adjust your program as you go.

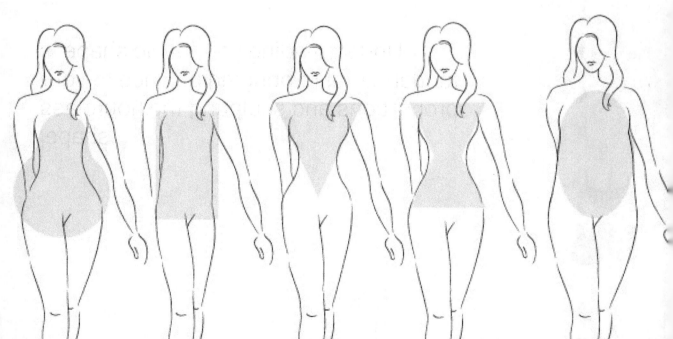

The *Hourglass* shape

Turn to page 101 if this is you

Balanced shoulders & hips

Narrow waist
Waistbands may often be too large due to the defined waist

Rounded bottom and hips

The
Hourglass
shape

The Inverted Triangle shape

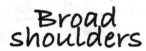

Broad shoulders

Narrow hips

Not much difference between the width of the hips and waist

Flat bottom

Wears a larger size garment on top half vs bottom half

Turn to page 84 if this is you

The

Pear

shape

Narrow shoulders and smaller bust

Wide hips and thighs

Wears a larger size garment on bottom half vs top half

Turn to page 77 if this is you

The
Ruler
shape

Smaller bust

Straight up
and down
shape

No clearly
defined waist
curve

May present an
ahthletic appearance

Flat bottom

Turn to page
89 if this is
you

The

Apple

shape

Rounded
shoulders

Round and full
mid-section

Narrow hips

Flatish bottom

Gains weight
in the belly and
breasts which
can mask your
shape

Turn to page
95 if this is
you

"

Wake up . Work out

Look *hot*

Kick *ass*

Rebalance your
Pear

shape with some sexy shoulders
and a streamlined waist

Mainstream fitness programs will tell you to lose weight and train legs often to tone up and shrink your hip dominant pear shape.

This advice makes me cringe because this is not how you bring symmetry to your proportions, in fact this approach can exaggerate the imbalance in your proportions. Let me explain.

It is likely that your lower body dominant shape is created by a combination of hip structure and body fat storage.

How fat loss *affects* your shape

As you may already be aware, body fat cannot be spot reduced. This means that any reductions in body fat will come from all over, including your upper body.

Reducing body fat is a great start, and will be included in your program, however, body fat reductions alone will simply result in a smaller pear shape. To demonstrate this further, please take a look at the illustration opposite.

While this is only a digital representation and your body is obviously unique to you, it is sufficient for the purposes of demonstrating what the underlying structure of a leaned down pear shape could be like.

As you can see, while this is a beautiful shape overall, the shoulders appear rather weak in comparison to the wide hip structure.

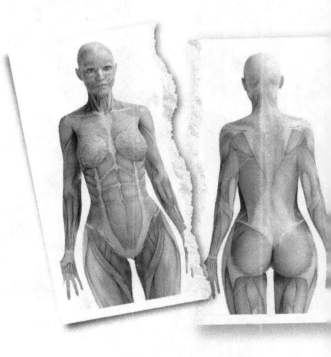

Working with your hip *Structure*

Your hip structure cannot be changed, even with drastic surgery because this is your genetic bone structure.

Rather than working against your dominant feature, I'll show you how to work with your already sexy shape.

How to do it
Focus on the *upper* body

The process of reshaping a pear shape to give the illusion of an hourglass is to build the upper body. By focusing on this area, you'll achieve the illusion of a smaller waist and hips.

Frist are your shoulders. Think back to the shoulder pad era. Pads were popular because they gave this exact illusion. Essentially, you will be building some muscular shoulder pads, but far better looking.

In addition to broadening your shoulders, you'll bring some width to your upper back, particularly the Latissimus Dorsi (lats) muscles

♥ Train muscles of the UPPER body regions often and with weight HEAVY enough to build muscular size (8-10 reps)

♥ Train muscles of the LOWER body regions less often and with LIGHTER weights that will define without building size (15+ reps)

Over on the following page is an example illustration of the amazing transformation this can make, so I hope you are as excited as I am. Are you ready? Great, then proceed...

Pear transformed to
hourglass

**Broader shoulders
+ Wider lats
= *Sexy* hourglass curves
and a whittled waist**

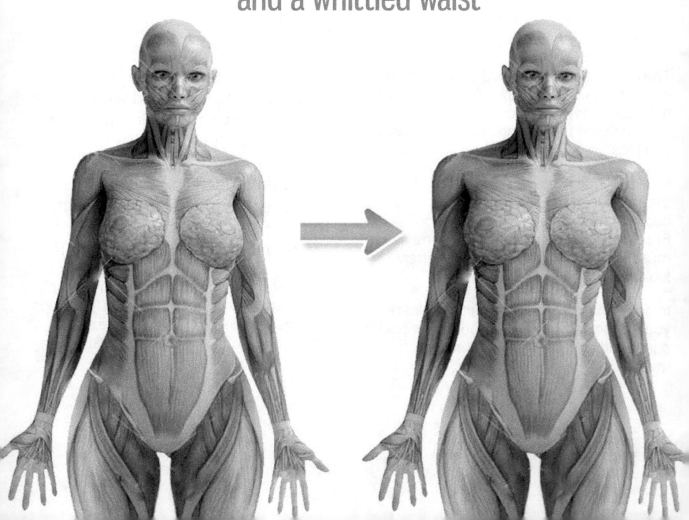

Pear transformed to *hourglass*

Broader shoulders
+ Wider lats
= *Sexy* hourglass curves
and a whittled waist

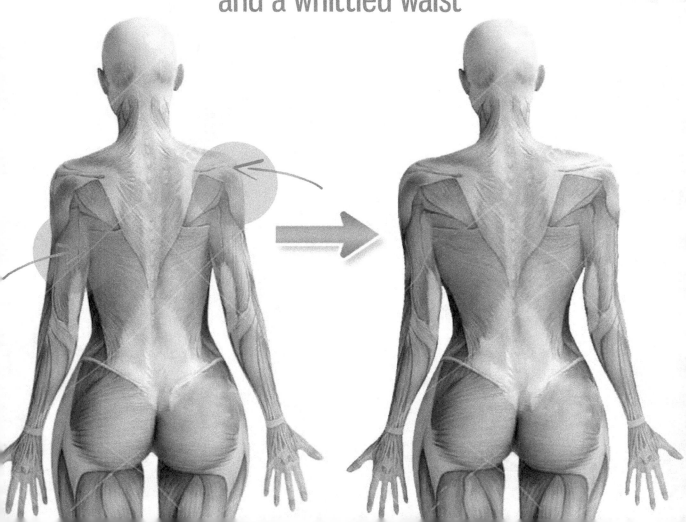

As a pear, you are more fortunate that you may realise. Building the lower body can be difficult for a lot of people, but you already have a great foundation to work with.

Even better, the upper body tends to respond faster to weight training than the lower body, which means you'll be looking hotter than you already do **very quickly.**

And don't worry, by training your lower body with lighter weights, you'll still sculpt a bombshell booty and killer legs,.

Watch out hot stuff.!!!

Want a program designed for you?

I have created a specialised training program for pear shapes:

The DreamCurves™
Upper Body Rebalancing Program

You can find out more by visiting us at
www.DreamGirlFitness.com

and as a valued DreamGirl member, you'll receive **10% off** when you use the code: LOVE10

Rebalance your

Inverted Triangle

shape with some killer legs and
some gorgeous glutes

You have a great *asset* to work with

There are many reasons why your upper body is well developed in comparison to your lower region. It could be due to having a wider bone structure or it could be due to muscular development. In either case, it is not something that can be changed.

But don't worry because having broad shoulders is a great asset to work with when sculpting out an hourglass shape, so rather than attempting to minimise their appearance, I'll show you how to work with those *sexy* shoulders.

How to do it
Focus on the *lower* body

For your shape, the key is to **build up your lower body.** This will bring a sense of balance and symmetry to your proportions and make your waist look utterly amazing.

The great news for you is that you already sport the most athletic shape, so the process of reshaping an inverted triangle shape to give the illusion of an hourglass is simply to:

♥ Train muscles of the LOWER body regions often and with weight HEAVY enough to build muscular size (8-12 reps)

♥ Train muscles of the UPPER body regions less often and with LIGHTER weights that will define without building any size (15+ reps)

Your program should include lots of **booty** and **leg** training.

Over on the following page is an example illustration of the amazing transformation this can make, so I hope you are as excited as I am.

Inverted Triangle transformed to *hourglass*

Broader quads
+ Boosted booty
= *Sexy* hourglass curves
and a whittled waist

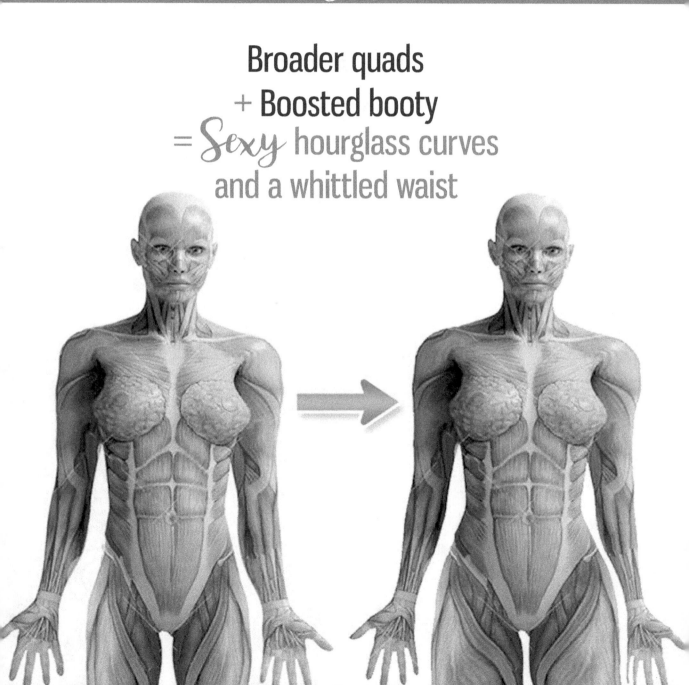

Inverted Triangle transformed to
hourglass

Broader quads
+ Boosted booty
= *Sexy* hourglass curves
and a whittled waist

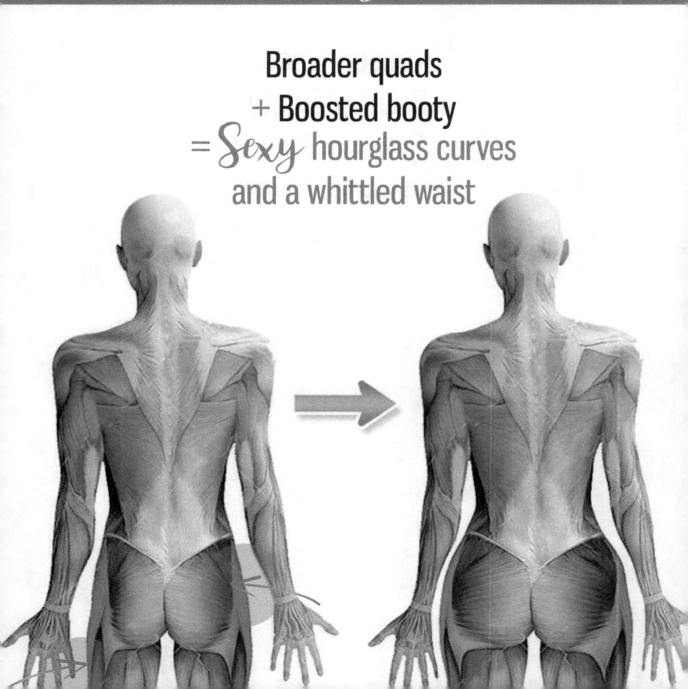

Want a program designed for you?

I have created a specialised training program for inverted triangle shapes:

**The DreamCurves™
Lower Body Rebalancing Program**

You can find out more by visiting us at
www.DreamGirlFitness.com

and as a valued DreamGirl member, you'll receive **10% off** when you use the code: LOVE10

"

Skinny Girls look good in clothes

Fit Girls look good

Naked

Add curves to your

Ruler

shape to create a feminine
and sexy body

You have a great *foundation*

As a ruler shape, you're going to be lacking curves, however, you're likely also sporting a very athletic and slim look to go with it, which gives a great foundation.

The priority for the ruler shape is going to be in bringing out all the curves associated with the feminine form, particularly your glutes, quads, lats and shoulders. Bringing shape to those areas will cinch your waist in, creating a curvier appearance.

How to do it
Focus on the *Upper* and *Lower* body

For your shape, you'll work simultaneously on developing your whole body, with emphasis on:building up your glutes to bring out your beautiful back curve, building out your shoulder deltoids and lats in the upper back to further cinch your waistline, and build your quads to further create the illusion of a shapelier waist curve.

You'll be lifting within the moderate-heavy weight range, which will bring out your curves and rebalance your composition, making you look toned and sexy.

The great news for you is that you already have a slim structure, so the process of bringing out those curves is through targeted training techniques that will involve:

♥ **Train muscles of the UPPER and LOWER body regions often and with weight HEAVY enough to build muscular size (8-12 reps)**

Your program should include both **upper** and **lower** body training..

Over on the following page is an example illustration of the amazing transformation this can make, so I hope you are as excited as I am.

Ruler transformed to
hourglass

Broader shoulders + Broader quads
+ Boosted booty + Wider lats
= *Sexy* hourglass curves
and a whittled waist

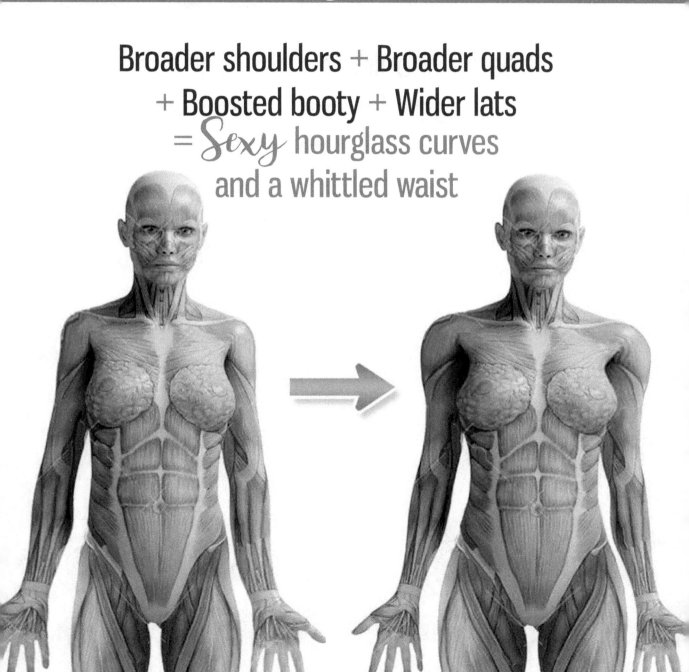

Ruler transformed to
hourglass

Broader shoulders + Broader quads
+ Boosted booty + Wider lats
= *Sexy* hourglass curves
and a whittled waist

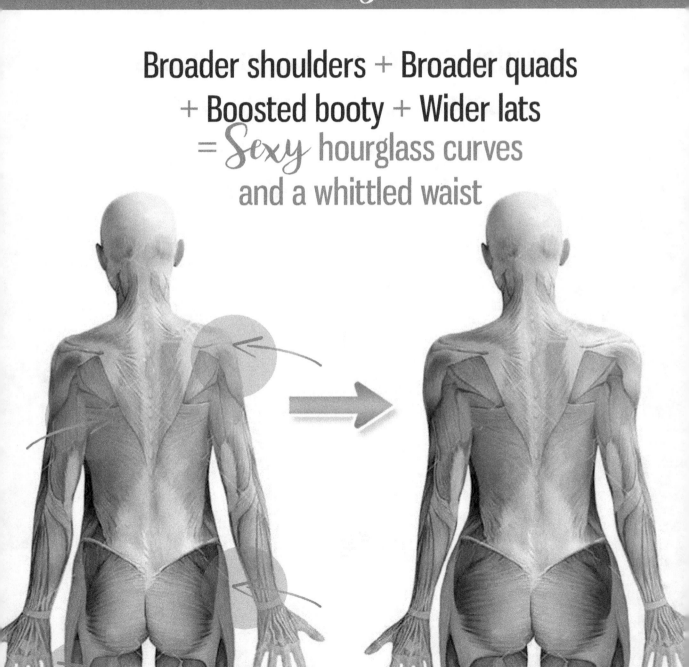

Want a program designed for you?

I have created a specialised training
program for ruler shapes:

The DreamCurves™
Signature Body Transformation Program

You can find out more by visiting us at
www.DreamGirlFitness.com

and as a valued DreamGirl member, you'll receive **10% off** when you
use the code: LOVE10

"

It's not about

having time

It's about

making time

Transform your

Apple

shape and cinch
your waistline

You'll see *quick* results in your mid-section

An apple shaped body has a tendency to carry much of the fleshy bits around the midsection, giving the torso a rounded appearance. There are actually several reasons why this may occur, including: Hormonal imbalances, body fat accumulation, bloating and water retention

The bad news is fat accumulation in the mid region is a health risk, but the good news is that **you'll see your waist reduce very quickly** when you begin to implement the correct dietary and exercise components. In fact, this program will be of highest value to an apple shape because of the shear increase in health benefits you will enjoy.

Trust me, you'll be sporting a flat tummy in no time. To bring balance to your shape, you'll want to first focus on reducing overall body fat and bringing balance to your hormones.

How to do it
Focus on *reducing* body fat and *balancing* your hormones

Because your shape is likely to be distorted by your swollen mid-section, you'll see much greater results if you first focus on reducing the volume. You can do this by following a healthy eating plan, performing fat burning cardio and looking at any hormonal imbalances.

To sculpt your curves, I suggest starting out on full body training using the following: approach

♥ Train muscles of the UPPER and LOWER body regions often and with weight HEAVY enough to build muscular size (8-12 reps)

Once your mid-section is reduced, you change your approach if necessary.

Apple transformed to
hourglass

Reduced volume in the mid-section
+ Developed upper and lower body
= *Sexy* hourglass curves
and a whittled waist

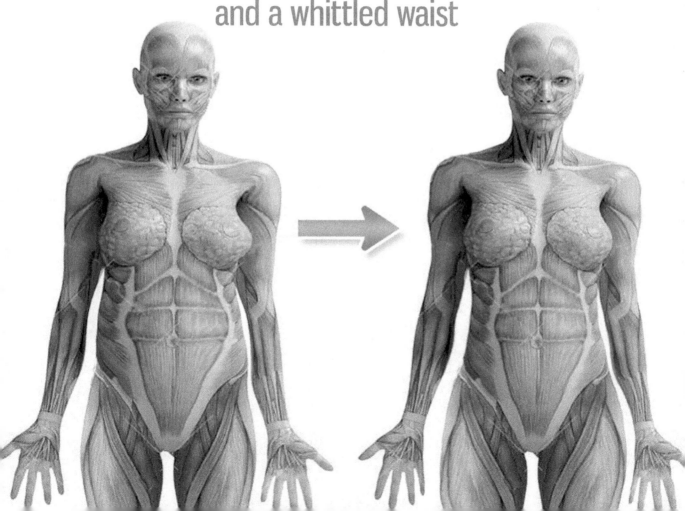

Apple transformed to
hourglass

Reduced volume in the mid-section
+ Developed upper and lower body
= *Sexy* hourglass curves
and a whittled waist

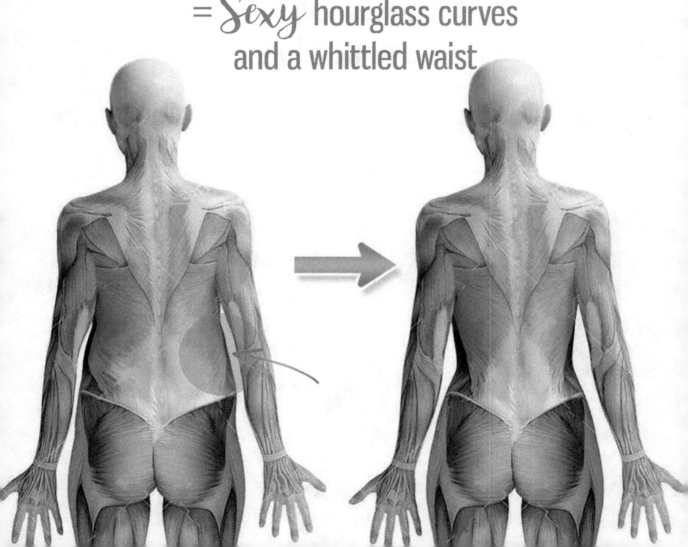

Want a program
designed for you?

Unless you can clearly see that you have an imbalance in your upper or lower body region, I suggest starting out with the Signature program. Once the area around your torso has reduced, you can switch to another program if necessary., but this is a great all round program suitale for most body types.

The DreamCurves™
Signature Body Transformation Program

You can find out more by visiting us at
www.DreamGirlFitness.com

and as a valued DreamGirl member, you'll receive **10% off** when you use the code: LOVE10

"

The best project
you'll ever work on is

You

Enhance your sexy

Hourglass

shape and make it even curvier

As an hourglass, you already have the curvy foundation, so you'll not have to perform any rebalancing. Instead you can focus your energy and attention on enhancing what you already have and addressing your overall body composition. You lucky thing.

How to do it
Focus on *reducing* body fat and *enhancing* your curves

For your hourglass curves, you'll work simultaneously on developing your whole body, with emphasis on:

♥ **Building your glutes to further enhance your beautiful back curve**

♥ **Building your shoulder deltoids and upper back to further cinch your waistline**

The great news for you is that you already have a curvy structure, so the process of bringing out those curves is through targeted training techniques that will involve:

♥ **Lifting within the MODERATE to HEAVY weigth range, on both the UPPER and LOWER body regions which will rebalance your body composition and make your curves even more defined (8-12 reps)**

Hourglass transformed to an even sexier and curvier *hourglass*

Broader shoulders + Broader quads
+ Wider lats + Boosted Booty
= *Sexier* hourglass curves
and a whittled waist

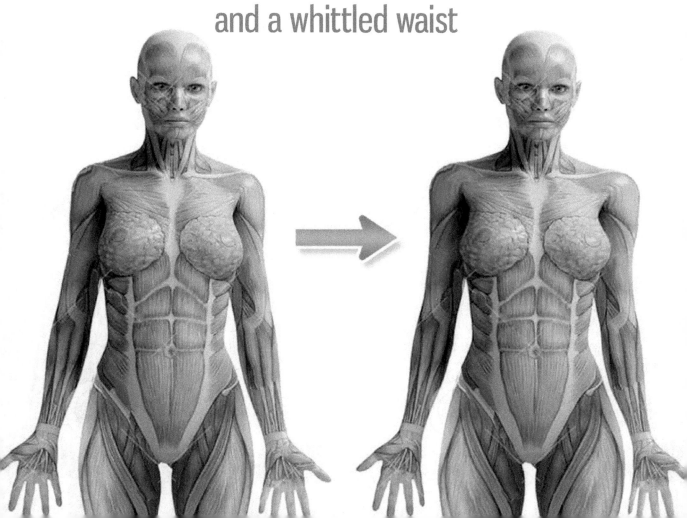

Hourglass transformed to an even sexier and curvier *hourglass*

Broader shoulders + Broader quads
+ Wider lats + Boosted Booty
= *Sexier* hourglass curves
and a whittled waist

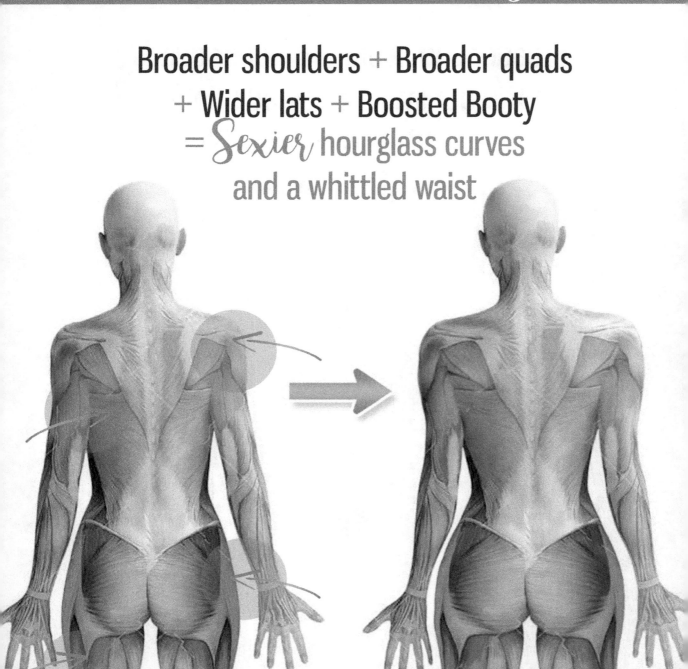

Want a program designed for you?

Our signature program is ideal for enhancing your curves, to create the sexiest shape ever. You are already gifted with curves, so you already have genetic potential for stepping on stage or becoming a fitness model. So check out the:

**The DreamCurves™
Signature Body Transformation Program**

You can find out more by visiting us at
www.DreamGirlFitness.com

and as a valued DreamGirl member, you'll receive **10% off** when you use the code: LOVE10

Fat gain creates an apple or pear shape

The more fat you gain, the wider your hips, thighs, butt and waist become, giving you an endomorphic apple or pear shaped body.

Fat loss tends to create in a skinny ruler shape

The more fat you lose, the smaller those areas become and you develop a narrower body with low levels of curves.

Targeted muscle building creates an hourglass shape

The more muscle you build, the bigger the muscles in your butt, shoulders and legs become, bringing out the curves that create an hourglass shape even while fat is reduced.

The bottom line is *build muscle*

When you build the muscles that are synonymous with the hourglass shape, you'll maintain that shape even after the fat is reduced.

No muscle = no shape when fat is reduced.

Oh, but we're not done yet. Now we're going to look at targeted training techniques in detail. Starting with, the gorgeous glutes.

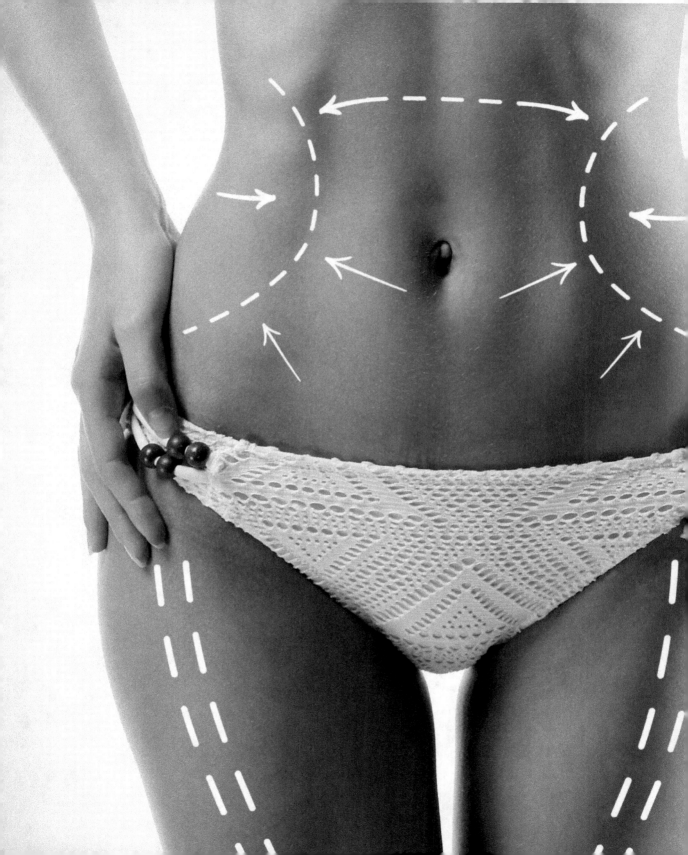

"
You don't get the *ass* you want by sitting on it

Sculpt a

Bombshell

booty that'll turn heads

The *glute* muscles

The gluteal region is made up of *three* distinct muscles, these are:

- ♥ Gluteus MAXIMUS
- ♥ Gluteus MEDIUS
- ♥ Gluteus MINIMUS

To create a firm and round derrière, it is essential that all three angles are targeted in your booty training.

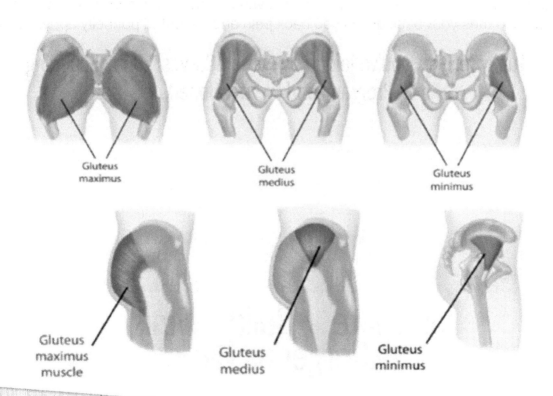

Gluteus maximus

Gluteus medius

Gluteus minimus

Gluteus maximus muscle

Gluteus medius

Gluteus minimus

The problem is - inactive *glutes*

The problem is, many people have inactive glutes due to weak gluteal muscles, poor form, dominant quads, or sitting all day.

What happens when glutes are inactive is the surrounding muscle groups begin to kick in to compensate, in this instance it is predominantly the quads, hamstrings and lower back.

Over time, those compensating muscles begin to develop and grow, but your glutes won't. This leads on to a disproportionate ratio of overdevelopment in compensating muscles and **the glutes looking smaller and smalle**r.

Not ideal if you are looking to develop a sexy hourglass shape. Worse still, over time this leads on to problems with your posture. Your toes start pointing outwards and your knees begin to cave inwards. Your hips tilt forward which then hyper extends your back giving you back pain and a bloated pot belly appearance.

Lucky for you, you've joined the DreamCurves™ Body Sculpting Program, and I've developed...

The Dream Girl
Bombshell Booty Formula

ACTIVATE > BUILD > FINISH

Activate + Build + Finish = Gorgeous Glutes

I've been there

After wearing high heals for many years of my life and working at a deskbound job, **I had weak and inactive glutes**, which led onto the worst case of back hyper-extension. I didn't even know this was a problem until someone pointed it out to me, but I've managed to use the bombshell booty formula to strengthen and build my glutes, and now you can too.

These are my results from using the DreamGirl Bombshell Booty Formula. These are not enhanced in any way, this is my genuine booty transformation.

Activate

The best way to re-engage and isolate your glutes is to use glute activation exercises on a regular basis.

Glute activation exercises are isolation movements that make it easy to engage the glutes without too much interference from compensating and surrounding muscles.

They get blood pumping into the area and re-establish the mind-muscle connection.

Use them as a warm up prior to performing your main booty session and you'll get the most bang for your buck.

If after introducing glute activation exercises, you still find your quads dominating your movements, you may find quad exhaustion exercises work well for you.

Simply throw in some leg extensions and leg presses (feet close and low on the plate) into your activation circuit. These will fatigue your quad muscles and inhibit their tendency to take ove.

ACTIVATE

Pre *activation* exercises

Following are some sample activation circuits that will get your glutes firing on all cylinders.

These exercises are done rather quickly, but with good form. Each rep should be around 1 second in duration, and the entire warm up should take around 3 minutes to complete.

The circuits shouldn't be heavy or intense, but feel free to use latex bands, cables or light weights if you feel the benefit is greater.

Circuit one

Banded sumo walk
Banded kick backs
Banded bridges

Circuit three

Banded seated or lying clams
Assisted pistol squats
Banded pull throughs

Circuit two

Frog pumps
Banded step out squat
Kettlebell swings

Circuit four

Kneeling squats
Banded low squat pulses
Banded three way lunges

Glute Bridges

Kettlebell Swings

Kneeling Squats

Banded Sumo Walks

BUILD

Start with some *compound* work

With your glutes activated and your quads exhausted, you'll want to swap out the bands and load up with some iron.

To get the most bang for your buck, start your booty session with a couple of compound movements. Compound movements will hit several muscle groups in one go, therefore building strength in your entire body and **burning a tonne of calories.**

Here are some examples of what you could include:

Compound Booty Exercises

Leg presses (Feet wide and high on the plate)
Reverse lunges (Step backwards into the lunge)
Bulgarian split squats (Back foot elevated on bench)
Reverse hack squat (Facing the machine)
Ball squats

Ball Squats

Reverse Lunges

Bulgarian Split Squats

Hit your *booty* head on

Remember what I said about the three glute heads... Isolated exercises is where you can target each of those and build that killer derriére

Isolated moves are what will give you the rounded and firm booty, without too much additional quad development.

First, let's look at exercises that target the biggest muscle, the glute maximus. Some of the best performing isolated movements for the glute max are outlined below, but hip thrusts in particular are like gold dust for your glutes, and should be included in abundance throughout your training.

Select 1-2 exercises from the list and say hello to the sexiest booty !!!

Gluteus Maximus Exercises

Hip thrusts (Shoulders elevated on a bench)
Cable Pull through
Kickbacks (Cables, Smith Machine etc)
Glute focused hyper extensions

Hip Thrusts

Pull Throughs

Kickbacks

Hyper Extensions

Get the 3d effect

The next set of exercises are designed to target the medius and minimus muscles, creating the rounded 3D shape.

So, you've hit your legs and booty with your compound movements, you've hit your glute max head on, and now it's time to shape the sides.

Select one or two exercises from the following list

Some of these are also compound movements which overlap, so mix and match accordingly.

Gluteus Minimus & Medius Exercises

Reverse hip abduction (Face the machine)
Cable hip abduction
Plié squats (Legs wide)
Curtsy lunges (Back leg travels laterally)
Wide and high leg press

Curtsy Lunges

Cable Hip Abduction

Plié Squats

The *finishing* touches

To bring the booty session to a close, finish up with a burnout circuit.

These will deplete any remaining energy from your glutes and help in the mind muscle connection.

Burnout exercises use the same exercises you have performed within your activation circuits, using the same speed and resistance. You'll perform them for about 3 minutes until your glutes are depleted and that wraps up the session.

You can use the same circuit you used to activate your glutes, or use a different set, the choice is yours.

A quick note of caution

Performing activation and exhaustion exercises will fatigue your muscles faster than usual. As a result, you won't be able to handle the same weights as you would without their inclusion, and you may find it a little more challenging to keep your form and balance.

Don't be afraid to go lighter, use a spotter and use machines in place of free weights for support if necessary. Stay safe!!!

You'll also find that after using finishing exercises, your glutes will be thoroughly fatigued when you leave the gym, so don't be surprised if you can barely walk upright. It's a good sign you've done a great job. Enjoy the feeling of a job well done.

SOME *tips* TO ENHANCE YOUR SESSION AND YOUR *booty*

Squeeeeeze

When performing a glute exercise, always focus on contracting your glutes as much as possible throughout the entire range of movement, especially at the top of the movement.

It sounds obvious but it's so important that it deserves to be emphasised

Always keep the following key points in mind when performing a glute exercise:

♥ Always brace your core

♥ Drive through your heels to get the glutes involved

♥ At the top of each movement, hold for 1-2 seconds as you squeeze your glutes hard then give a quick pulse

!!! The squeeze at the top of the movement is much more important than the weight !!!

Squeeze your glutes whenever you remember, every day. Squeeze them when working at your desk, when preparing meals, when walking up the stairs, etc. Every opportunity will increase your rate of growth that much more.

HIT YOUR GLUTES *hard* AND HIT THEM *often*

The glutes take time to build and can handle frequent loads, so you'll want to train them often and go hard.

To get maximum growth, your glutes must be trained at sufficient intensity.

Bodyweight exercises are perfectly fine for activating the muscles depleting the last bit of energy, or between sessions, but your glutes need to be put under heavy loads and often if you are to develop a firm and round booty.

With optimum weight and frequency of training, you'll get great results.

Ideally you'll work your glutes 2 or even 3 times a week. In each session you could change the rep range to cover all basis, for example:

- Day one: 4-6 reps
- Day two : 6-8 reps
- Day three : 8-12 reps

You could do your HIIT's and sprints in the same session to avoid overlap, but it all depends on how much you've depleted your glutes. The choice is yours, but it is an option to consider.

WEIGHT IS IRRELEVANT, *form* IS KEY

Focus on *form*

Form is vital for avoiding pain and injury, and keeping the appropriate contraction.

When lifting heavy, only lift as heavy as you are able to maintain correct form. As soon as form begins to suffer, pause and readjust your position or weight if necessary.

Health always comes first.

NEWBIES *listen up*

If possible, seek the assistance of someone who can demonstrate the exercise and correct your technique. This will help you learn and progress much quicker, and avoid potential injury.

Once you have the form mastered, start experimenting with the weight to find the right volume for you.

With the form mastered and correct volume, you can really start to make some serious progress.

Concentrate on *foot placement*

Adjusting your foot placement when performing certain movements will alter the stress loading pattern.

In English, this means that differing foot placements places different muscles under stress.

For targeting the various muscles within the glutes, use the following feet positioning:

♥ **Leg press**
High and narrow (glute maximus) or high and wide (glute medius and minimus)

♥ **Free weight squats**
Go wide

♥ **Smith machine squats**
Feet wide and forward

And **always** drive through your heels.

Feet high on foot pad	Feet Standard	Feet apart, toes out	Feet close
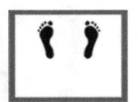	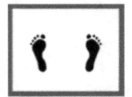	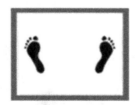	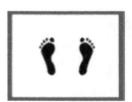
Emphasis on glutes and hamstrings	Emphasis on Quadriceps as a whole	Emphasis on inner thigh region (adductors)	Emphasis on outer thigh region

A HUMBLE AND INEXPENSIVE
latex band

Latex loop bands, or any other sort of resistance band for that matter, is my all time favourite tool of choice. I have them in my kitchen, in my bathroom and take a variety of resistances to the gym with me. Why?

Using a resistance band, in addition to your loaded weights, will give you constant tension throughout the entire range of movement in your training, transforming your workout and, ultimately, your derrière.

They are inexpensive, portable, and convenient.

You can loop one around your ankle and perform some multi-directional hip abductors while doing your makeup or cooking dinner, hook one around your thighs while doing your household chores, or even around a piece of equipment in the gym to add that extra resistance. They are simply amazing.

"

Any idiot can drive
in a straight line
But it takes an
expert to handle
these

Curves

Whittle your

Waistline

and flatten your stomach

FIRST, WHAT TO *avoid*

IF YOU WANT A SMALL WAIST, AVOID *side bends* AND *oblique* TRAINING

When I go to the gym and see ladies performing oblique training or, worse still: weighted oblique training, argh, I just want to cry.

Such exercises are often included in fitness programs and many ladies mistakingly include them in their workout routines not realising that **these exercises increase the width and thickness of the waistline**, making the waist appear **boxy** and **bulked**, not curvy and streamlined.

If your goal is to get a curvy and streamlined waist, side bends that target the obliques should be avoided at all costs. Take a look at the illustrations following for a further demonstration of how disasterous such training can be to your feminine shape.

GOODBYE CURVES

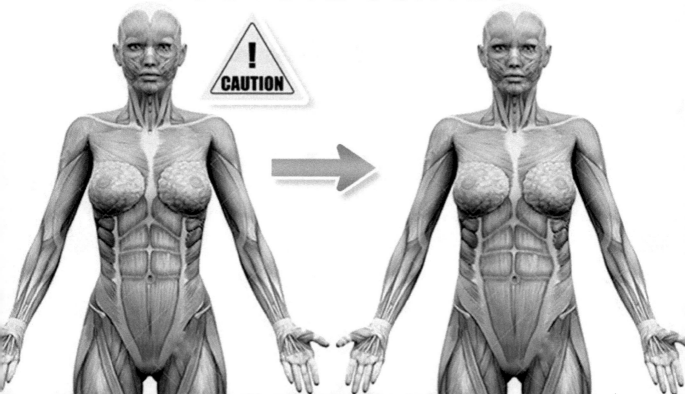

AVOID EXCESSIVE AMOUNTS OF
weighted AB TRAINING

Weighted ab training, and too much ab training in general, can lead to a thickening of the abdominal walls and a heavy six pack.

If you're looking for a more defined abdominal region, that is perfectly fine, however, these should be avoided if you want to create a feminine and streamlined abdominal region.

Take a look at the illustration following and see the difference between highly developed abs versus a strong core without much development.

It all depends on what your goals are.

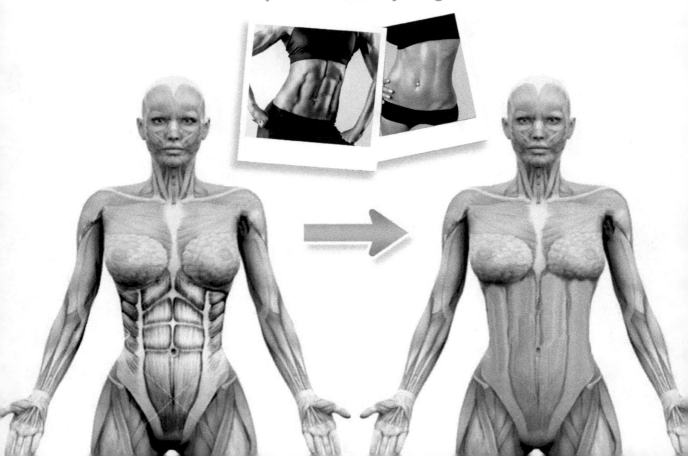

MAKE EVERYTHING ELSE
bigger

Yup, you read that right, and no I'm not crazy.

Allow me to explain the power of illusions and how using them to your advantage will get you the sexiest, womanly curves you can ever imagine. just take a look at the illustrations below, amazing right. And that's before we've tried to shrink and tighten the waist itself.

THE POWER OF ILLUSION

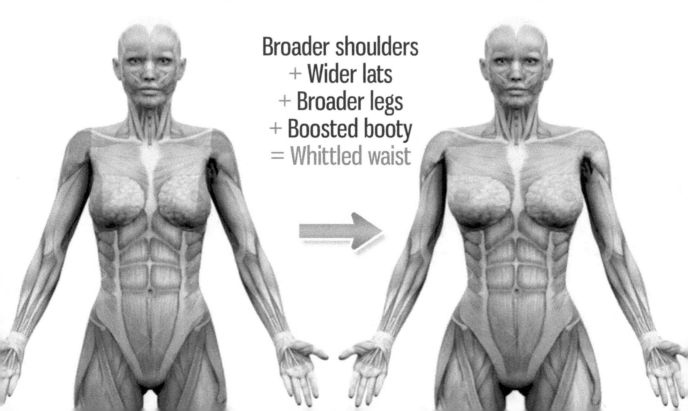

Broader shoulders
+ Wider lats
+ Broader legs
+ Boosted booty
= Whittled waist

NO *extremes* NECESSARY

JUST BEAUTIFUL *sexy* CURVES

All I have done to create these curves is give a little boost to the booty, widened the legs, lats and delts. You don't need to have any ribs removed, no organs donated, and you certainly do not need to do tonnes of ab work, if much at all.

With only some slight adjustments to your frame, you can create some very sexy looking curves and the illusion of a very tiny waist, without even altering your waist.

The targeted training techniques you have been introduced to in the previous sections, and those coming up, will recreate this for you and your body shape in real life, so I hope you are excited.

But wait, we're not done yet. Continue reading to learn more.

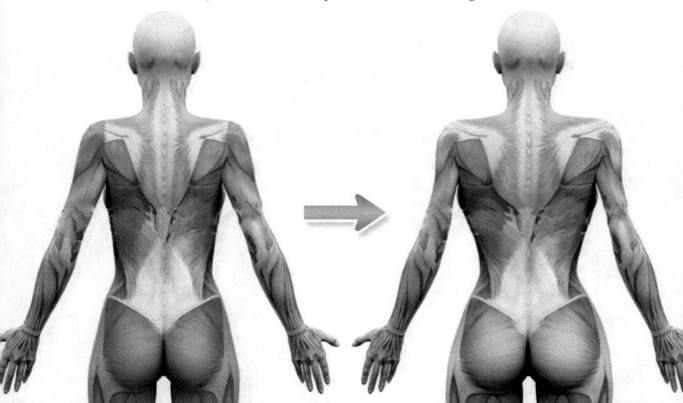

GET *slim* FOR BEST RESULTS

Aim for 15-20% BODY FAT

Many ladies fall into the trap of overtraining their abs in the hopes of achieving a flat stomach, but a flat stomach doesn't come from abdominal exercises, it comes from reducing your body fat levels. **It really is that simple.**

This is why the DreamCurves™ program recommends limiting any direct abdominal work to only once a week, and focuses on bringing body fat levels within the 15-20% range. Within this range and development, you will see some lovely feminine definition, but not a highly chiseled six pack.

If you do want a highly chiseled six pack, just go against everything I say on this subject.

10-12%

15-17%

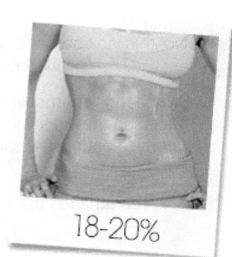

18-20%

MINDLESS *movements* ARE NOT MY THING

By now you must be thinking that I am against training the core, but this couldn't be further from the truth.

I am all for building a strong core, but I believe in doing the right exercises, with the right intensity and the right frequency to achieve the desired aesthetics. Mindless movements that bulk out the curves are not my thing.

There is one abdominal exercise that trumps all others for creating a beautifully defined and flat tummy, and has no thickening side effects.

This is the stomach vacuum.

No, this isn't some form of drastic liposuction, although the results can be just as impressive when used consistently.

Stomach vacuums work to build a strong internal abdominal wall, while keeping the external muscles small and feminine. They are also very convenient as you can do them anywhere, sitting, standing, kneeling or lying.

Top athletes use them to achieve a small waist, and so do we.

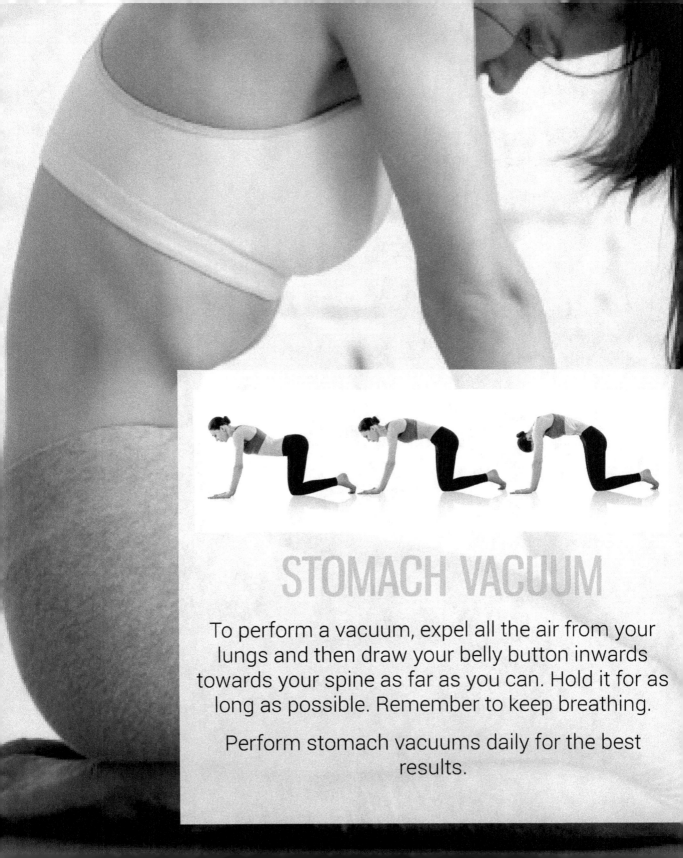

STOMACH VACUUM

To perform a vacuum, expel all the air from your lungs and then draw your belly button inwards towards your spine as far as you can. Hold it for as long as possible. Remember to keep breathing.

Perform stomach vacuums daily for the best results.

PERFORM *isometric* MOVEMENTS

ISOMETRIC EXERCISES ARE *forward* AND *backward* MOVEMENTS

Once a week, you'll also want to perform a few select isometric exercises. These work the frontal wall only and are ideal for keeping the core strong, but tight. Some great isometric movements are:

- Crunches
- In and outs
- Decline sit ups
- Flutter kicks
- Hanging leg raises

- Reverse crunches
- Sliding knee tucks
- Mountain climber
- Ab roller

You could also include planks

Hanging leg raise

Reverse crunches

In and outs

Mountain climbers

USE A WEIGHT TRAINING BELT TO KEEP YOUR CORE *tight* AS YOU TRAIN

It is important to wear a weight lifting belt whenever you touch a weight to keep your waist tight and stop the overdevelopment of your obliques.

These belts will minimise the contraction of your external abdominals during heavy lifts which would otherwise begin to engage. Not wearing a belt during training could, over time, increase the thickness of your waist by as much as an inch or more.

Another benefit to wearing a weight belt is that they make your internal abdominals work harder and this will develop internal core strength, but without the bulking out the external abdominals. **A win win you could say.**

Wear the belt snugly, but not so tight that it cuts off circulation or prevents contraction. When wearing the belt, do not push your stomach against the belt, as this will engage and thicken the external abdominal muscles. Also keep your core stable, do not allow yourself to slack.

If you want an even smaller and streamlined waist, you can choose to wear a waist trainer, however, I will tell you from the get go that waist trainers are controversial and some people entirely disagree with their usage.

I'll explain the reasons a little further and you'll be able to decide for yourself if this is something you'd like to try.

141

SHOULD YOU WEAR ONE *or not?*

It goes without saying that there are immediate visible benefits from waist trainers. You will see an instant reduction in your midsection and gain added postural support, however, it is the longer term use and results that I will cover here.

THE *good* POINT OF VIEW

When worn consistently and correctly, a waist trainer can lead to a waist circumference of half an inch to one inch smaller and a more streamlined shape. The way this works is by eliminating the engagement of the core muscles, which then leads to decreased muscle development and atrophy of the abdominal walls. And that is where part of the controversy and potential problems can occur.

THE *bad* POINT OF VIEW

Decreased use of the abdominal muscles can lead to a weaker core, and a corset that is worn too tight or aggressively can lead to lower bad pain, decreased blood flow and even squashing of your organs.

AND THE *facts*

Here's the thing, doing anything drastic or to extreme will reap negative side effects, and this is true for waist trainers too. So, the key to wearing one without the associated damage is to do so with the correct knowledge and application. I hope to share that with you on the following pages, but I also want to note that your judgement is essential.

Don't listen to nay-sayers, and don't even listen to me. Back up your decision with research and facts and then own your decision..

JUST HOW *tight* SHOULD THE TRAINER BE?

When you first receive your trainer, it will be tight, but it should not ever be extreme. Listen to your body and use your judgement.

You should be able to fasten the very top and bottom hooks and work you way down the rest with relative ease. If you have to use a second pair of hands or use a horse and carriage to stretch it to death, it's too small and you should get a larger size.

HOW SHOULD IT BE *worn* AND FOR *how long?*

If you don't have any allergies to latex, wear the shaper touching your skin. otherwise wear over a tank top or undergarment.

Start with light usage, wearing it as long as you feel comfortable. Gradually and slowly begin to increase the length of time you wear it, or take regular breaks, ultimately working up to wearing your trainer for 8-10 hours per day.

Consistency is key if it is going to be effective.

HOW TO CHOOSE A *trainer*

Select a trainer with a minimum of two rows of hooks and eyes. Make sure it has steel boning and is high quality. Cheaper variations will tear and pucker easily.

A latex trainer with cotton lining is great for day to day use, and a workout trainer can be worn during exercise.

Measure your waist and consult the size chart for proper sizing. Do not guess. I suggest ordering two trainers. one in your current size, and one a size smaller.

"

When you feel the weight of the world on your shoulders Get to the gym &

sculpt them

Sculpt Sexy
Shoulders
that look great in
any outfit

SHOULDERS ARE THE *missing* LINK

BUT ALSO THE MOST UNDER-RATED

Building your booty and cinching your waistline will not create the perfect hourglass silhouette without some broad, shapely and uber sexy shoulders to match

The shoulders are a largely under valued muscle that, not only plays a key role in creating balanced proportions, but also in giving the illusion of a smaller waist.

Yep, they are a vital asset in your quest for curves.

Unless you have an inverted triangle shape with naturally broad shoulders, I suggest training your shoulders at least twice weekly so that you can build out their structure. The goal is to bring them in line with the width of your hips or more and create a sexy sweeping curve to your arm profile..

The length of your shoulder bone will be a factor, however, well developed deltoids can give the appearance of wider and sexier shoulders.

The shoulder muscle is called the deltoid

JUST LIKE THE GLUTES, THE DELTOID HAS *three* HEADS THAT MAKE UP THE STRUCTURE

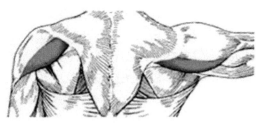

Posterior Deltoid

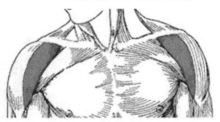

Anterior Deltoid

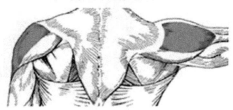

Medial Deltoid

These heads are:

♥ The Anterior (front delt)

The anterior head creates a 3D effect at the front, defining the transition between your shoulders and your chest.

♥ The Medial (side delt)

The medial head brings width and fullness to your upper body, creating balance and the illusion of slimming your waist.

♥ The Posterior (rear delt)

The posterior head brings shape and curve to your side profile, pulling your shoulders back, enhancing your posture, and boosting your bust

All three heads need to be developed to create full and balanced shoulders, and all three in balance will produce the sexiest and shapeliest profile.

SOME *important* TIDBITS

FOR INJURY PREVENTION AND EFFICIENCY

Always keep the following key points in mind when performing any shoulder exercise

♥ Always take a recovery day between chest and shoulder training sessions to prevent injury and fatigue.

♥ Avoid using swinging momentum. Keep your movements controlled.

♥ Avoid rocking your body to assist you in moving the weight. If you are struggling, consider decreasing the load or seek a spotter.

♥ Go through the full range of movement, no partial movements

♥ When performing lateral movements, tilt thumbs forward slightly.

♥ When performing upright rows, elbows should be higher than your hands

♥ **Try to avoid shrugging as this will engage your traps, rather than your deltoids. You don't want to develop your traps.**

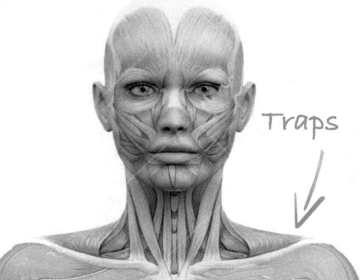

Traps

APPROVED SHOULDER *exercises*

THAT WILL SCULPT ALL THREE HEADS

- ♥ SHOULDER PRESS
- ♥ LATERAL RAISES
- ♥ ARNOLD PRESS
- ♥ FRONT RAISES

- ♥ REAR DELT RAISE
- ♥ STANDING CABLE REVERSE FLY
- ♥ HIGH ROPE REAR DELT PULL
- ♥ UPRIGHT ROW

Upright row

Front raise

Shoulder press

Bent over rear delt raise

High rope rear delt pull

Lateral raises

"

The time to transform your body is now

It's time to get

fierce

Say buh-bye to

Saddlebags

and muffin tops forever

So now that we've covered how a body recomposition process works and other factors which may be contributing to fat accumulation in your abdominal region, we're ready to delve into the subject of fat loss.

As you may already be aware, there are many flawed and faulty fitness programs on the market, and the problems with these is that they don't care if weight is coming from fat, muscle or water, and don't care if your metabolism is hampered in the process because they want you to lose weight quickly.

So I'm going to show you how an efficient fat loss process works and how to do it without sacrificing your muscle and without entering into starvation mode during the process.

But first, let's take a quick look at why traditional approaches fail and leave you stuck in the cycle of skinny fat syndrome.

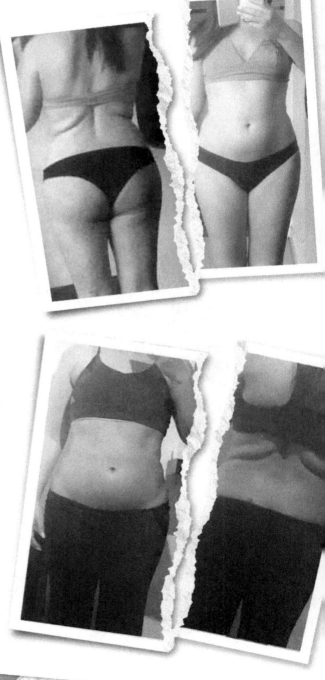

TYPICAL *fat loss* RESULTS

Real results

16 WEEKS PROGRESS

High calorie deficit, no carbs, lots of low intensity cardio daily and no weight training.

Body fat reduced, but low levels of muscle resulted in a soft appearnance that lacks tone and definition

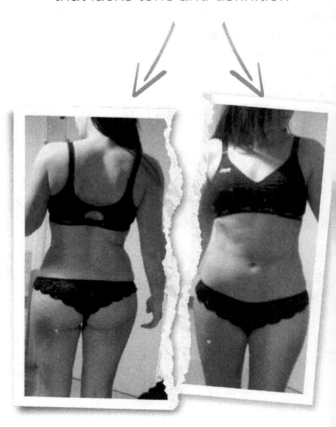

Real results

16 WEEKS PROGRESS

Moderate calorie deficit, carb and calorie cycling with weekly cheat meal, short HIIT cardio sessions, and 5 days weight training.

Body fat reduced, and muscle maintained resulting in a firm body.

Most approaches to fat loss begin with a calorie restriction, so let's take a brief look at what happens in a typical calorie restricted cycle.

When you restrict your calorie intake, your body fat will reduce, however, after some time your metabolic rate slows and so does the rate of fat loss. This is referred to as metabolic down-regulation.

There are two reasons why this happens: First, your body is smart and when it senses a limited food supply, it panics. Second, as your body fat reduces, your body will attempt to hold onto what's left, and this is partially due to a hormone called Leptin, but essentially this is just how our body's survival mechanism works

Once this down-regulation happens and fat loss slows, it is typical for a dieter to reduce their calories further.. As your body has already down-regulated your metabolism, reducing calories further not only serves to promote a further down-regulation, but because the calorie deficit is already severe, your body will start to enter starvation mode in order to prepare for potential famine.

The more severe the calorie restriction, the more your body down-regulates, the less fat your lose and... you get my point.

IT'S A *vicious* CYCLE

Start

Eat less

Pick a diet

Lose some fat

Resolve to try again

The Familiar Diet Failure Cycle

Keep going

Give up

Fat loss slows

Lose impetus

Have a blowout

Plateau

Your body is super smart and, in this state, your body will start to break down muscle tissue as it's preferred source of energy. Why? Because muscle burns more calories than fat, and your body is now in preservation mode and muscle is a threat.

Now when you weigh yourself, muscle wasting is typically what's reflected in the weight lost and the skinny fat cycle has begun.

UNFORTUNATELY, IT GETS *worse*

As you're aware, most people don't stop at a simple calorie reduction for fat loss, nooooo, they add hours of gruelling cardio into the mix, unaware of the damage and devastation they are causing their body.

THAT'S WHERE THINGS GET REALLY

THE RECIPE FOR *disaster*

Cardio itself is not the problem, cardio while in a severe calorie deficit is the problem because your body is already in a compromised and muscle wasting state. Adding cardio in this instance is just counterproductive as your body will use muscle for fuel to sustain it's energy requirements during the activity, as well as further down-regulating your metabolism to hold onto the body fat you still have.

And if that's not yet bad enough, there's also the addition of fad dieting principles to contend with too. Yikes. In the 80's it was low fat, today the media has just made everyone afraid to eat at all. Fats and carbs are seen as fattening and protein makes you too big.

IT'S ALL A BUNCH OF *balony*

Without going into too much detail and causing your brain to down-regulate, let's just say that it's a vicious downward spiral from this point and you could do your body a lot of long term damage, both at a metabolic level and a hormonal one.

HERE'S THE RECIPE FOR *disaster*

A SEVERE CALORIE DEFICIT plus LONG CARDIO SESSIONS
plus INADEQUATE NUTRITION plus NO WEIGHT TRAINING
RESULT = METABOLIC DISASTER

The good news is, there's a better and more efficient way to approach fat loss and that's what I will now teach you.

RIGHT *tools* WRONG *strategy*

You've heard the best way to boil a frog is to do it slowly, right? Well, fat loss works on a similar principle. If you throw all your fat loss tools into the mix all at once and at maximum intensity, alarm bells will ring causing your metabolism will down-regulate and fat loss to stall.

On the other hand, if you incrementally and strategically increase the intensity of those tools, your metabolism will not perceive danger and will continue to release those fat stores.

You see, all those techniques and tools outlined do work, and each has their place in a fat loss program, but it's how they are used that will determine the eventual outcome.

THE ELEMENTS THEMSELVES ARE NOT FLAWED IT'S THE APPROACH THAT IS

In order to release body fat, you need to be in a calorie deficit, you need to do some cardio, and you will need to manipulate your nutrition, however, how much of a calorie deficit, what volume and type of cardio, and how you distribute your nutrients is the key that will determine whether you lose body fat or muscle, and whether your metabolism remains strong, or suffers.

Think of baking a cake, yum. You can use the right ingredients, but add the ingredients in the wrong order and the outcome can be very different. As someone who struggled with cooking for a long time, I know this all too well.

So, let's take a look at the recipe for fat loss I have found to work extremely well.

CALORIES ARE *key*

FIRST, CALCULATE YOUR CALORIES CORRECTLY

If you take a look around the internet, there are many calorie calculators and each seem to throw back a different result, leaving most people bewildered. Worse still, many of those underestimate how many calories you need, and any deficit you introduce on top of an already low number is far too severe.

There's one formula of calorie calculation that I use and find is the most accurate, and that's the:

Harris-Benedict formula

This formula works so well because it takes into consideration your gender, age, height and weight, but also your activity levels. I have created a calculator for calculating your calories based on this method, and you can download it by visiting the DreamGirl website. (www.dreamgirlfitness.com/caloriecalculator)

USE A MODERATE DEFICIT RANGE AND CYCLE IT

In order to bring your body fat levels down, I suggest using a conservative calorie deficit between 15-20% below maintenance, and using that deficit on a rotation basis whereby you eat more on training days than you do on rest days. This means that those calories will be partitioned where they will be used and not stored. For example:

Training day = 15% deficit
Rest day = 20% deficit

BUT USE THEM *correctly*

WANT *faster* RESULTS?

If you have a special occassion coming up and really want to trim down for that, you can increase your deficit range temporarily, but I don't suggest it for the longer term.. 8 weeks is the max I would go for within this range.

In this instance, I go with:

Training day = 20% deficit
Rest day = 25% deficit

In order to come out of this heavier calorie deficit without any rebounding effects, all you have to do is increase your calories back up to the 15 and 20% calroie deficit range outlined previously This will help your body come out of the deficit witout any rebounding weight gain, but you'll also continue to lose body fat because you'll still be in a deficit. This is a method referred to as reverse dieting and is a great tool to use any time you have been in a calorie restriction.

HAVE REGULAR *cheat* MEALS

Your body is smart and, any time you are in a calorie deficit, it will begin to adapt. As your body fat begins to reduce, so does the hormone leptin, and there is a potential for your body to panic itself into starvation mode if the deficit is sustained for long periods. Starvation mode is especially messy, and you'll want to avoid that as much as possible, and the great news is that a regular cheat meal can help you do just that.

There are so many benefits to having a cheat meal, but the greatest is that it will also enhance your results. This is because before your body ever percieves that you are in a deficit, the cheat meal will spike those calories back up. This is what will keep your body burning those body fat stores and prevent a fat loss plateau. Bon apetit.

MANIPULATE THE TIMING OF YOUR

carbohydrates

If you have a low carb breakfast, your body will turn to fat for fuel at a higher percentage throughout the day than if you have a high carb breakfast. This is because having high carbs for breakfast will leave your body using those carbohydrates for fuel for much of the day.

Conversely, after exercising at a high intensity or weight training, your muscle glycogen stores become depleted, therefore making your muscle cells highly receptive. This is the best time to introduce carbs into your meal plan.

USE *carb* CYCLING

Eliminating carbohydrates is not necessary, but you can manipulate your intake of them to assist you in reaching your goals and eliminating uneccessary demands for insulin production. So, just like how you would rotate your calorie intake on training and rest days, you can do the same with your carbs. This is commonly termed carb cycling.

During a fat loss program, I recommend:

Training day = 20% of your daily calorie intake
Rest day = Veggies only

BUMP UP YOUR *protein*

As your body gets leaner, the more likely it is that your body will turn to muscle to satisfy it's energy requirements. Protein is the key to preserving your muscle and keeping your body turning to fat for its fuel, so it is essential to have an adequate amount in your diet. Protein also has a high thermic effect, whcih means you'll burn more calories simply by digesting and processing it than with any of the other macronutritents, so protein is a win win.

During the fat burning phase, keep your protein to at least 50% of your daily calorie intake.

Protein intake = 50% of daily calories

HAVE PROTEIN BEFORE *cardio*

If you intend to do any form of fasted cardio, it is essential to have a source of protein before or during your cardio session to prevent muscle breakdown. BCAA's are ideal for this purpose, or you could use a whey protein if that is more convenient.

DO THE RIGHT *activities*

DO HIIT CARDIO SESSIONS FOR ALL OUT
fat burning

Checking in for a long and boring snooze session on the hamster wheel 7 days a week is not the most efficient way to burn body fat. Sure long runs are great for your fitness level, but they aren't so great for all out fat burning. And forget the fat burning zone, that's clever marketing at work.

Say hello to HIIT training and say hello to a lean and sexy body.

By far the greatest benefit of HIIT over low intensity cardio is it's ability to preserve muscle while it burns huge amounts of body fat. Longer sessions of cardio are proven to be more likely to burn muscle for fuel, which only serves to preserve the skinny fat cycle. Better still, HIIT cardio continues to burn calories for up to 24 hours after your session, and that's how the fat burning effects are amplified.

Time = 15-30 minutes
Frequency = 2-5 days

You'll want to be in and out in no more than 30 minutes.

Because the body adapts and becomes more efficient over time, you'll want to increase the duration and/or intensity every 2 weeks. Once you are hitting 30 minutes and cannot possibly go faster, increase the elevation or resistance, or increase your frequency.

If you want to learn more about how to incorporate resistance training into your fat loss program, or would like to have a program already created, please vist the DreamGirl website.

SCULPT THOSE *curves*

LIFT SOME *heavy* WEIGHTS

One of the most overlooked tools for reducing body fat, particularly among us females, is heavy weight training.

Lifting heavy weights **causes your metabolic rate to skyrocket**, and it'll transform your body like nobodies business. Forget low weight and high reps as they'll do nothing for your composition or your curves.

Don't be afraid to go heavy with weights because that is what will sculpt out your curves and give you that firm beach body look. If you haven't read the section on skinny fat syndrome, please read through it now to understand why weight training is so important.

As mentioned previously, cardio and a calorie deficit alone will result in muscle loss and the skinny fat syndrome, and this is why heavy weight training is even more crucial during a fat loss program than any other time.

Weight training = 3 days a week minimum

During the fat loss phase, train with weights for a minimum of 3 days each week. 4 days are better than 3 and 5 days are better than 4, but do what works for you and never do less than 3 days.

Rep range = 8-12 reps
Sets = At least 3 per exercise

If you want to learn more about how to incorporate resistance training into your fat loss program, or would like to have a program already created, please vist the DreamGirl website.

AVOID *Rebound* FAT GAIN ?

Once you have lost the body fat, what next? How do you stop the rebound effect?

USE

REVERSE ⟳ DIETING

Reverse dieting is just how it sounds, you reverse the dieting process.

So, where you would incrementally decrease your calories to lose the body fat and avoid hitting a plateau, now you will incrementally increase those calories back up to your maintenance to avoid putting excess body fat back on. It's a technique used by fitness models and athletes, and it's the missing link from most diet and fat loss programs.

Now you may be thinking that as long as you raise your calories back up to maintenance you wont' put on body fat, but this isn't the case and is the mistake may people make after being on a restricted program. Hence why many pile back on the lbs.

The reason reverse dieting is so incredibly effective is because as you lose the body fat, your body downregulates your metabolism. Because your body has adapted to those lower calories and the slower metabolism, reverse dieting allows your body to gradually adjust back up to your new maintenance.

Think about it like this, when your body fat is low and you've been in a calorie reduction, your body is sensitive and would love nothing more than to bring those body fat stores back up. It's how the in built survival mechanism works.

With the reverse dieting process,you give your body the food it needs, but in a controlled manner .

KEEP AT *it* AND REAP THE *Rewards*

AVOID DAMAGING YOUR METABOLISM AND HORMONES

If you can resist the temptation to revert to old habits and see the reverse diet through, not only will you maintain your new beautiful lean body, but you'll also avoid damaging your metabolism and will keep your hormones balanced.

How to do it

If you have been on a 20 & 25% calorie deficit, start by reducing that deficit to 15 & 20% levels for 1 to 2 weeks.

Keep your weekly cheat meal too, this is crucial.

After this 1-2 weeks, reduce your calorie deficit further to the 10 & 15% mark. Do that for another 1-2 weeks. Then keep dropping the deficit every 1-2 weeks to the next increment until you hit your maintenance.

You'll also need to scale back your HIIT training, so swap out your HIIT's for heavy weight training instead. This will keep your metabolism fired up so you don't put any excess body fat on, but will also prepare you to transition into the Sculpt phase where you can work on building your muscles and sculpting those sexy curves.

Once you hit maintenance calories, the level where you are not gaining or losing any more body fat. I'd suggest staying there for a few weeks to allow your body to rest and recover. Enjoy your new body for a while.

Then, when you are ready, you can progress full steam ahead into sculpting some curves for your new leaner body.

"

Dear Fat,

Prepare to *Die*

Sincerely

Me.

Muffin Tops

and Love Handles

muffin top and love handles

Could be caused by an imbalance with your *hormones*

While an imbalanced body composition is the major factor creating a smoothed appearance, **it's not the only factor.**

The soft and flabby appearance that is associated with skinny fat syndrome, and the accumulation of abdominal fat deposits that give you a muffin top or love handles, could be symptomatic of an underlying hormonal imbalance.

The most likely of those are:

- ♥ **INSULIN RESISTANCE**
- ♥ **HIGH LEVELS OF INSULIN PRODUCTION**
- ♥ **ELEVATED CORTISOL LEVELS**

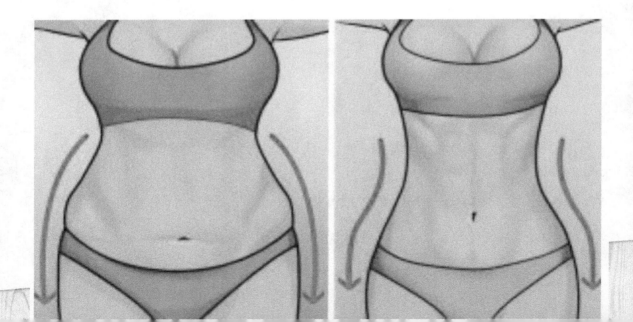

Sugar
and Insulin

Insulin is a storage hormone. It's job is to transport sugar from the bloodstream to your cells where it can be

USED FOR FUEL or STORED AS FAT

Your cells respond well to small amounts of insulin, but problems can occur when the body releases chronically high levels.

When this happens, this storage process becomes inefficient and sluggish and insulin resistance can occur. If you suffer from muffin top you'll want to look at lowering your insulin spikes and increasing your insulin sensitivity.

This can be achieved by manipulating one or all of the following:

+ Exercise
+ Nutrition
+ Supplementation

I am a *chocoholic*

I've always suffered from back fat, even while I was at my leanest, why? because I spent most of my life over-indulging in the sweet stuff. During high school and into college, my diet consisted of chocolate and chicken - in that order.

For years I didn't understand how to get rid of my pesky back boobs because I didn't understand hormones or their effects on my body.

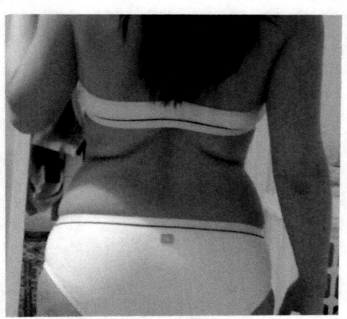

The result of being a chocoholic

Manipulate your
carbohydrate intake

Many insulin resistant individuals make the mistake of reducing carbohydrates to drastic levels or eliminating them entirely. Unfortunately, this doesn't address the underlying problem, but can actually **make the problem worse**. Not to mention the hampering effects on muscle development.

Obviously carbohydrates do play a role here, but that isn't to say that they should be avoided. Rather, it is better to use them according to your needs so that you can control the release of insulin during times when they are most needed.

HAVE CARBS AROUND YOUR

training

On training days when your energy needs are increased, introduce carbohydrates around your training where they are primed for use, especially after your training where they can replenish glycogen stores and increase protein synthesis.

This is also the best time to have higher GI or sugary carbs because you'll want the insulin spike to shuttle protein to your muscle cells quickly.

LOWER CARBS ON *Rest days*

On rest days when you are mostly sedentary, your needs for energy are much lower. As such, taking a low carb day on rest days can avoid unnecessary demands for insulin production.

STICK TO LOW GI *carbs*

Sticking to low GI carbs will slow the release of insulin. GI refers to the glycaemic index and indicates the effects particular foods have on your blood sugar levels.

Foods such as white rice, white bread, white potatoes, white pasta, chocolate and bananas are high on the glycaemic index and need to be limited as much as possible.

Combine YOUR CARBS

Eating carbohydrates in isolation will cause insulin to spike.

You can reduce this effect by combining them with foods that increase insulin sensitivity. Here are some of the best additions you can make:

- ❤ **Vinegar** increases glucose uptake by the muscle cells
- ❤ **Protein** slows down the absorption rate of carbs
- ❤ **Fibre** reduces absorption of carbs
- ❤ **Fish oils** mimic insulin and enhances glucose metabolism
- ❤ **Cinnamon** with your meals reduces fasting insulin levels and lowers glucose
- ❤ **Green tea** with meals, may inhibit the production of glucose, preventing blood sugar spikes.

Increase uptake of *glucose*

GET *active* AND BUILD MUSCLE

Strength training and high intensity cardio activity demands high levels of glucose for energy. This demand utilises glucose at a faster rate, increasing glucose uptake by your muscles. This, in turn, improves insulin sensitivity as the body doesn't need to produce as much insulin to clear the glucose from the bloodstream.

This can continue for upward of 24 hours following your workout.

In addition, as you increase your muscle mass, your storage capacity for glycogen also increases, thus becoming more efficient.

- Increase your muscle to increase storage capacity

- Perform high intensity cardio and weight train to burn glycogen stores

- Take regular breaks and remain active

HERE ARE SOME *other* THINGS

- ♥ Eat more veggies
- ♥ Avoid drinking large amounts of alcohol
- ♥ Have apple cider vinegar before bed
- ♥ Avoid liquid fructose, high fructose corn syrup and agave
- ♥ Supplement with magnesium
- ♥ Avoid restrictive dieting

Note: If you have diabetes, please seek appropriate medical advice before starting DreamCurves or any other program.

Stress
and Cortisol

Not only can too much cortisol lead to health problems if sustained, it can also totally ruin your beautiful hourglass shape by allowing fat to take shelter right on your curves.

The good news is, while fat cannot be spot reduced, a muffin top caused by stress can be controlled.

So what is cortisol?

Cortisol is a stress hormone that is released under situations of physical, mental, emotional and environmental stress.

Before you close this document and declare that you are not stressed and this is not relevant to you, hear me out because there is more to stress than losing your temper with that annoying jerk who just cut you up in traffic or feeling peeved by your annoying boss.

The causes of stress

Stress occurs in many forms, even in those that you may not suspect, such as:

- 💜 **Exercise**
- 💜 **Lack of sleep and exhaustion**
- 💜 **Anxiety and depression**
- 💜 **Extreme dieting and skipping meals**
- 💜 **Stimulents, such as caffeine and alcohol**
- 💜 **Digestive issues and inflammation**
- 💜 **Bright lights and technology**

Some levels of stress are perfectly fine and can even assist the body, providing extra strength and alertness.

The problem occurs when stress is chronic and sustained as these can be detrimental to your health and body composition.

... and the *effects*

When your body experiences stress, it realeases cortisol and adrenaline in preparation for action. This is known as the flight or fight response.

As well as increasing your heart rate and blood flow, this response releases glucose into the bloodstream.

Now, if you've read the guidance on insulin you've already realised what effect this will have. When glucose is in the bloodstream, insulin is released to transport it to cells. Over time, chronically elevated levels can cause the following problems:

- ❤ **Slower metabolism**
- ❤ **Increased fat storage**
- ❤ **Loss of lean tissue**
- ❤ **Increased appetite and cravings**
- ❤ **Impaired digestion and inflammation**
- ❤ **Abdominal fat**
- ❤ **Slow cell regeneration**
- ❤ **Weak immune system**

BE AWARE OF THE
symptoms

After a stress induced cycle, blood sugar levels can plummet and crash, leaving you craving sugar and stimulants. So, next time you find yourself craving something sweet or feel like you need a boost, it could be due to stress.

Drink water, go for a short walk, use deep breathing exercises and relaxation techniques and see if the cravings subside. Fuelling up on sugar or stimulants will only fuel the cycle.

BEWARE OF STRESS INDUCING
stimulants

Caffeine releases adrenaline and, therefore, stress. Use in moderation and avoid if under any undue stress. Caffeine can be found in chocolate, fizzy pop, tea, and coffee. Alcohol is another stimulant that increases stress levels, so reduce and moderate consumption.

TAKE TIME OUT TO
relax and unwind

Participate in some low intensity and fun activities outside of your training. You could spend time with your friends taking dance classes, do yoga classes, go for a spa session or massage.

Be sure to get plenty of rest and reduce your time in front of technology, especially in the hour before bed.

While this all seems like obvious and mundane advice, sometimes it takes some reminding. I'm a workaholic, so I certainly need some reminding from time to time.

"

The process
doesn't need to
be
complicated

Taking the die

Out of Diet

"

If at first you don't succeed, fix your

ponytail

and *try again*

Eat cake

and drop body fat

Get creative with your meals

When done right, you truly can have your cake and eatit.

Don't believe me? Then take a look at the meal plan below and you'll see a meal plan I used personally to drop my unwanted body fat during my competition prep. Tell me if you think that's bland and boring. I rest my case...

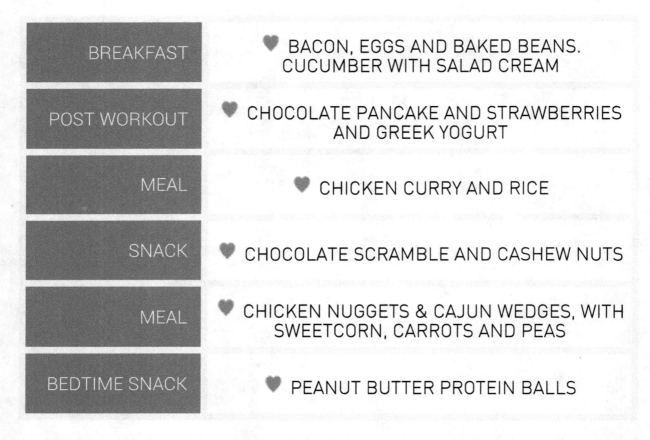

BREAKFAST	♥ BACON, EGGS AND BAKED BEANS. CUCUMBER WITH SALAD CREAM
POST WORKOUT	♥ CHOCOLATE PANCAKE AND STRAWBERRIES AND GREEK YOGURT
MEAL	♥ CHICKEN CURRY AND RICE
SNACK	♥ CHOCOLATE SCRAMBLE AND CASHEW NUTS
MEAL	♥ CHICKEN NUGGETS & CAJUN WEDGES, WITH SWEETCORN, CARROTS AND PEAS
BEDTIME SNACK	♥ PEANUT BUTTER PROTEIN BALLS

Meals don't have to be bland and boring to be effective on a fat loss program, it's all about being creative and swapping out some of the ingredients to make a meal that tastes amazing, but without spiking insulin levels or encouraging fat storage. Take a look opposite for some excellent food upgrades that will transform any meal into a healthy alternative.

GOOD

93% Lean ground beef
Light canned tuna
Duck
Veal
Cheese raw
Probiotic (lactose free)
Lentils
Peanuts
Banana
Romain lettuce
White rice
Instant oats
Rye whole grain
White potato

BETTER

Sirloin
Tilapia
Chicken
Lamb
Cottage cheese
Lactose free yogurt
Lima beans
Almonds
Apple
Spinach
Brown rice
Whole oats
Barley/millet/spelt
Sweet potato

BEST

Filet mignon
Salmon
Turkey
Bison
Egg
Greek yogurt
Fava beans
Walnuts
Blueberries
Kale
Quinoa
Steel cut oats
Sprout
Celeriac

Or make simple swaps

In addition, you could make simple adaptations to the ingredients within your favourite dishes to make a healthy alternative that fits within your program, but still tastes utterly amazing. For instance, take a look at these simple adaptations.

If your recipe calls for this		Try substituting with this:
Ground beef or lamb	»	50/50 mix with turkey
Sunflower oil or ghee	»	Olive or Coconut oil
Sugar	»	Stevia or honey
Cream	»	Natural yogurt or coconut milk
Cow's milk	»	Almond or coconut milk
Margerine	»	Butter
Couscous	»	Quinoa
Pasta	»	Spaghetti squash
Chocolate chips	»	Cacao nibs
Bread crumbs	»	Rolled oats
White flour	»	Wholewheat, almond or oat flour
Table salt	»	Himalayan sea salt
Sour cream	»	Greek yogurt
Mayonaise	»	Greek yogurt or hummus
Syrup	»	Pureed fruit
Bacon	»	Turkey bacon

Here's how I did it

With my meal plan on the previous page, here's how I made it work for me:

Bacon eggs and beans
Real bacon, 1 whole egg and 2 egg whites, and no added sugar baked beans

Chocolate pancake and strawberries
Recipe on the following page. You're welcome :)

Chicken curry and rice
Mix of white and brown basmati rice, chicken breast cooked in home made curry using olive oil and spice

Chocolate scramble
This is much more delicous than appearnaces suggest. Simply makde scrambled egg using some almond milk, 1 egg and 2 egg whites and mix in some cocoa powder. Delicious and no carb chocolately snack.

Chicken nuggets
Chicken breast coated in crushed almond nuts, with a light coating of olive oil and baked in the oven

Cajun wedges
Recipe to follow

Peanut butter protein balls
Recipe following

CHOCOLATE PANCAKE

Those meals on my plan are not difficult to create. All I've done to make them part of my fat loss program is switch out ingredients. For instance:

Here's how to make a delicious chocolate pancake:

INGREDIENTS

+ 50ml water or almond milk
+ 2 egg whites
+ 1/2 scoop vanilla whey protein powder
+ Cocoa powder to taste
+ 40g oats

INSTRUCTIONS

+ Blend the batter using an electric hand blender if you have one until a smooth consistency is formed.
+ Spray a frying pan with non-stick spray and cook on a low heat like a regular pancake.
+ Flip once and serve.
+ Grate some 90% chocolate over the top if you so desire and pair with a dollop of Greek yogurt for extra protein goodness

CHOCOLATE PEANUT BUTTER BALLS

INGREDIENTS

+ 1/4 cup peanut butter
+ 1 scoop vanilla whey
+ 1 1/2 tbsp salted butter, softened
+ 1/2 cup powdered stevia
+ 100g 90% chocolate

INSTRUCTIONS

+ Mix peanut butter, whey and butter together
+ Gradually stir in stevia until combined well
+ Cover and let sit for about 15 minutes
+ Shape into 1-inch balls, place on a baking sheet, cover and refrigerate for at least 20 minutes to allow to firm up.
+ Dough balls should hold shape before dipping in chocolate. Add more refrigeration time if necessary.
+ Melt chocolate and dip peanut butter balls one at a time
+ Place on waxed paper lined baking sheet, cover and refrigerate until ready to serve.

CAJUN CELERIAC WEDGES

INGREDIENTS

+ 1/2 Celeriac (approx 300g)
+ 1tsp Paprika
+ 1/2 tsp Garlic Powder
+ 1 tsp Olive Oil
+ A sprinkling of Rosemary
+ Salt to taste

INSTRUCTIONS

+ Pre-heat the oven to 400 degrees f (gas mark 5)
+ Peal and cut celeriac into wedges
+ Place into a pan of cold water and bring to the boil
+ Once the water has been bubbling for a couple of minutes, drain the fries and place them on a baking tray. Allow the steam to evaporate.
+ Blend the oil and seasonings and brush over the wedges until covered
+ Roast for about 45 minutes, flipping the wedges half way, until the outside of the wedges turn golden brown and crispy on the edges and the inside is tender.

"

Nothing tastes as good, as being slim

feels

AND THAT'S HOW *bikini* BABES
SCULPT *fierce* BODIES

Of course that's just a brief overview of how the process works, and there is more to it that is beyond the scope of this book, but hopefully it clarifies some of the confusing and conflicting information that is floating around out there.

Put some of the advice in this book into practice and see the changes take place in your own body. It is possible to reverse skinny fat syndrome and metabolic damage using these techniques if you're willing to give it a try and let go of old ideas about cardio, scale weight and excessive calorie reductions.

Lifting weights creates a very sexy body with plenty of feminine and graceful curves when you use it appropriately. So don't be afraid of iron. It's going to change your body and your life.

Thanks for reading this guide. If you found it of value, I'm always grateful to hear your feedback, and would appreciate your review. This helps me make improvements for future updates.

CPSIA information can be obtained
at www.ICGtesting.com
Printed in the USA
BVHW011740020919
557367BV00007B/118/P